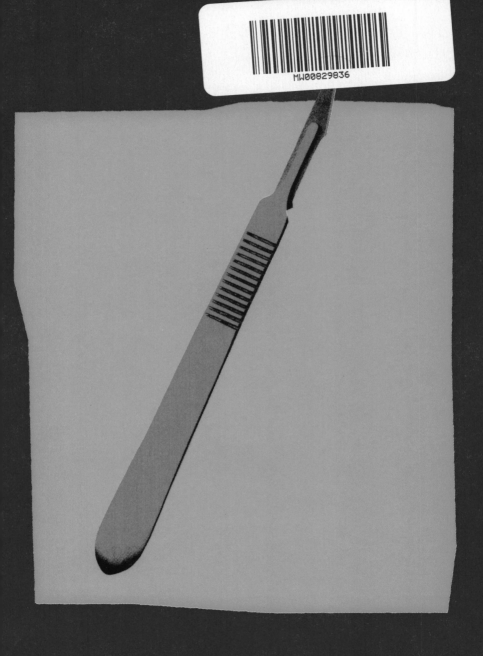

AUTOPSY

(of an ex-teen heartthrob)

AUTOPSY

(of an ex-teen heartthrob)

(poems of rage, love, sex, and sadness)

AVAN JOGIA

G

Gallery Books

New York Amsterdam/Antwerp London Toronto Sydney New Delhi

Gallery Books
An Imprint of Simon & Schuster, LLC
1230 Avenue of the Americas
New York, NY 10020

The names of some real people appear in this book, but they are applied to these poems in a fictitious manner.

First Gallery Books hardcover edition February 2025

GALLERY BOOKS and colophon are registered trademarks of Simon & Schuster, LLC

For information about special discounts for bulk purchases, please contact Simon & Schuster Special Sales at 1-866-506-1949 or business@simonandschuster.com.

The Simon & Schuster Speakers Bureau can bring authors to your live event. For more information or to book an event, contact the Simon & Schuster Speakers Bureau at 1-866-248-3049 or visit our website at www.simonspeakers.com.

Interior design by Jason Snyder

Manufactured in the United States of America

10 9 8 7 6 5 4 3 2 1

Library of Congress Control Number: 2024948804

ISBN 978-1-6680-6227-2
ISBN 978-1-6680-6229-6 (ebook)

To _____ ,
who, without their love, I would never
have been able to be so honest.

AUTOPSY

(of an ex-teen heartthrob)

Autopsia, n. To see for oneself.

Postmortem. Dead.
At least almost.
Or at the very least dying slowly.
Lying on a cold metal slab.
Having my insides poked at with a fork, or a scalpel.
Hell of a way to wake up. 32.
Having my guts prodded at with a spoon.
Makes you wonder why they call it the "Operation theater."
The performance of being picked apart by you,
all of you,
huddled around me with white gloves,
in white coats,
beady eyes shining out above your surgical masks, pale blue.
I'm woozy and disorientated,
having been under the anesthetic of too much
vanity, fame, love, lust, anger, sadness, shame, rage, fear, and booze.

Self-dissection.
I moved to LA when I was 18, born into a world I thought
    I understood.
Chasing my spark. Pursuing the dream.
But for reasons this book will explore, I became afraid.
I awoke into consciousness midway through my life.
Having already decided, in my youthful arrogance, on the
    direction my life would take.
Without first consulting my future.
I've spent the last few years rearranging the direction of my life.
Looking into myself in the only way you can.
Getting the scalpel out.
Writing.

For you.
Standing over top of me.
Staring down at my naked body.
Splayed.
Pulling at my intestines, tugging at my endocrine system.
The lacerations on my extremities.
Defensive wounds from trying to protect myself.
Or my cracked calvarium.
My brain spilling out with overthinking.
My heart's ventricles, unable to pump love through my veins
that have clotted and clogged with age.

I just hope that maybe you can see yourself in me.
In this body laid out in front of you.
In my skin, that you cut open with your scalpel.
Maybe what is ugly and what is beautiful in me is familiar to you.
Perhaps you recognize, in me, your own frustrations with the
world around you, that you too, feel hopeless and lazy and
enormous and chosen and full of love and of softness and yet
still feckless and broken, and maybe you see your part in all
this too.
Your vanity, fame, love, lust, anger, sadness, shame, rage, fear,
and booze.

Laid out on the cold slab in the operating room.

Anyways, Enjoy.

—A

good kids

We are Good kids
Showbiz kids
We give out hugs
Don't do drugs
Sell lunch boxes, stickers, and mugs
What _good_ kids!
Go tell your parents
We are your childhood
We are who raised you
No adolescence for the good kids
This is the life <u>YOU</u> chose
And it's not yours
<u>Such</u> good kids
Macy's Thanksgiving Day Parade
Behave
_J-14_
Teen Scene
Tiger Beat
Smile and wave
Win tickets to go and meet
The Real Good Kids
Kids' Choice kids
Teen idols
Suicidal
Tidal wave of guilt and shame
Rip the poster out and paste in place
The real _good_ kids

(2010)

The goons, with their million-dollar deals and desperate
    court appeals,
screwing hookers on Sunset and Vine, doing the minimal
    jail time,
movers, shakers,
liars, the Lakers,

LA breathes without a pulse, sustaining itself
on broken dreams,
cocaine,
and yoga.

The anorexic vegan actress drives her Prius
to audition for Topless Girl Number Two.
She's not going to get it,
doesn't have the tits for it.

Too short, too tall,
too dark, too bald,
too thin,
numbers, ratings, which demos tuned in,

who's screwing who or more importantly, who hasn't screwed her.
Producers, directors, and those goddamn talkers,
the side-smiling lawyers and the star-obsessed stalkers,
the Golden Globes, Emmys,
Cannes, and the Oscars.
It took him ten takes!
Did you make her an offer?

Dropped by CAA, picked up by Endeavor,
the script is in spec,
and everyone's under the weather.
Rewrite, retake,
another fucking remake,
enough with those for god's sake.
Boob job, nose job,
Botox, blow job,
did you hear that he's gay?
Really? I thought she went both ways . . .

Sleeping pills, a fifth of bourbon,
she's *just* white enough,
he's too urban.

Openings, screenings,
red carpets, premieres.
The studio loved it!
But here are their fears.

And to the cracked actor
with your store-bought bone structure,
know that soon,
silicone ruptures.

And when god in her heaven
sends the floods and the thunders,
your face on a billboard
will highlight man's blunders.

marathon runner

My mum got cancer the first week of me shooting The Show. Ovarian. I had just turned eighteen and she was down in LA with me when she found out. She immediately flew back to Canada; you know, free health care, and I was left under the supervision of the other parents on The Show. I know she is really thankful to all of them for looking after me. She would undergo a radical and intense surgery that would change her life forever, but she would live.

This event is interesting to me, so much life would happen in that short week. The Show that would change my life started filming. My accidental independence down in Los Angeles would begin, and I would first start becoming concerned with mortality's finite nature in a real way. I would feel real fear for the first time.

I was an incredibly confident child. Annoyingly so, by all accounts. It powered everything I did. I was so sure I was going to be an actor, and that I would be a writer and director, and that I deserved to, if you will forgive me, put my fucking dreams in action. Where my unwarranted confidence came from? No one knew; I certainly didn't. But it would break for the first time when my mum got sick. I would second-guess all of it. I would become unsure.

I would deal with this by becoming increasingly more unruly. I can see it for what it is now. At the time I thought I was just partying and setting myself on fire because I was young and was oppositional defiant. It was partly that, but more honestly, I was acting out because I was scared of the temporary nature of everything.

I was worried things wouldn't be perfect. That I would become some tragedy before my life had begun. Tragedy I would carry, like a stone in my shoe, the kind of sadness you can see in a person's eyes when they try to meet yours—the kind they try to hide when they quickly look away. I didn't want that kind of pain and most of all I didn't want to lose my friend.

So when I see The Show, I see a complicated time in my life, filled with lots of joy, growing up with my friends, the newness of what I was doing, but also so much fear. The unknown of life becoming real to me for the first time. I have never stopped being scared, I don't think. That is my great takeaway. I'm always scared. I have just learned to run right at it. I used to run at it in more toxic ways. Now I run at it by writing to you all. I run, I write. I run at it by reigniting my dreams and making art that I love even though it might fail and loving even though I might get hurt.

I am a fucking marathon runner now.

The man who goes into the burning building twice is truly brave, because he knows how hot the flames are. I learned to just keep going back into the fire. To run right at it.

bark, bark

I'm at the Cannes Film Festival being introduced to a famous dog.
The dog was invited by a jewelry company
to be at the opening of their new line of necklaces.
I feel like me and this dog understand each other.
We are both being carted around on a leash,
taking pictures with bullshit products we don't care about,
being asked very little about the film we've made,
which is the whole point of the festival.

He is more famous than me.
The dog.
To be honest, I don't even have a film in the festival.
I am just fucking around in France.

Am I willing to get down on all fours and bark?
Just to be invited to the product launch after-party of a movie
no one actually sat down and watched?

Bark bark, I guess.

the ego show

Ego is an interesting beast.
Without it I would feel untethered and defenseless.

It is a burden.
It is also a promise of safety.

"I am not going to let myself be nothing.
I won't simply kneel to those who would try to kill my spirit.
I am alive, I am human, and I matter."

But it is also a poison,
one you brew for yourself,
and you drink expecting others to fall ill.
It is callous,
green,
nauseous with envy and worthlessness.

Ego is The Sickness.

orange carpets

Orange carpets
And I'm an actor, remember?
Avan?
Do you remember?
Scuba diver
And a lunch box made of human skin,
Playing pretend for strangers,
And into the slime I go
With my scuba suit on.
"This is all just life experience,"
I tell myself.
"It'll make you a better scuba diver."
You're an actor, remember?
Act grateful.

Maybe this wasn't meant for you.
Sometimes you get gifted someone else's dream.
No bitterness, just an observation.
Wake up. Big smile.

I'm not a human being,
I just play one on TV.

idol hands

He leaned on lockers and ran his hands through his hair,
Professionally,
Like for a living.
His grandfather was a metalworker
And worked at a fucking plastics factory,
But all he did was smirk and say a few words.

[*Laugh track*]

It's easier work,
But leaves you feeling you didn't really make anything.
The soft hands of an actor.
Acting isn't soft work necessarily.
But the work he did was.
It left his soul and his hands weak and pliable.
Idol hands are the devil's playthings.
Comfort is the secret enemy of happiness.
He really just wanted to be used,
Effectively and well,
To a cause his soul found fitting.
This is the truest path to contentment,
To have a purpose that aligns with your values and dreams.
And to lose yourself to that purpose.

[*Laugh track*]

Now he knows the difference,
Between comfort and contentment,
And his hands will never be soft another day in his life.

the view from the kids' table

The view from the kids' table.
Looking over at the adults eating dinner,
You start to think they must know something you don't.
The conversation over there seems much more interesting.
But I've been sitting at the kids' table,
and I'm grown,
and my knees don't fit in my seat;
they bang the edge of the table and bruise.
"I want what they eat."

prayers of love and sadness

When I first started writing this book I was engaged to be married
    and in love.
Somewhere in the middle of its writing, I was alone again
and decided maybe I was going to be the kind of person
who finds meaning in friendships, lovers, and family.

Upon finishing this book, I am in love again.

These are my prayers to the saints of love and sadness.
The range of feeling I have felt within those two spectrums
and the understanding
that one doesn't exist without the other.

If you have never been sad, you never loved,
and if you aren't in love, you will never be sad.
But you'll be numb.

Avoid numbness at all costs.
to love and believe and be wrong is a privilege of a life set on fire.
Be baptized fully in the waters of that uncertainty.

tin rings

I lost the ring you gave me in the sea in Hawaii.
You got down on one knee
With a ring tab from a beer can
And with tears on your cheeks
You said,
"Will you please marry me?"
You were crying 'cause I said you reminded me of Patti Smith
And I guess you felt seen
And we had been fighting for weeks
And I admit, I was weak.

I lost the ring you gave me in the sea in Hawaii.
This tin ring of trust
That I knew would rust.
So I swore to adorn it with gold,
Plate it with precious metal
So it would never get old.
But the sea swept it up and it wore down to dust.
Another piece of junk
Scraping the sand
Along with our love.

I lost the ring you gave me in the sea in Hawaii.

blur person

When I was a child
and dreamt of my wife,
the type of child's dream you spend your whole life
making right,
I saw a woman beside me,
the lady of our house.
And she wears a dress I can just make out
as green
and we live in a castle of gray and of white.
I can see
that her lips are moving but I can't quite hear what she's saying
she vaguely sounds like she's praying
and our children run like wolves through the halls of our home,
swirling around us
through the grounds,
down the road,
And out of sight
And I think that she's looking at me
But her face is obscured
A blur of pure love
and of light.

Until I saw your face and it sharpened.

You are the Blur Person
from my child's dream.

I can see clearly that the dress you have on is of emerald—
your mother's, I believe.

And you're looking at me as your eyes start to well up,
but you don't seem to grieve.

And I can hear the words that your lips start to form.
The sound on my face like a breeze.

"I can see you,"
you say.
"I've looked for you my whole life,"
you say.
"You're not a blur to me now."

What relief.

blur person: part 2

You are a blur to me again
And I'm not sure if you ever wore green.

Our castle still stands,
Of gray and of white,
But it feels cavernous
And empty
And mean.

And our wolf cubs are nowhere to be seen.

I wander the halls of our castle
Like a blind king
Of some fallen and forgotten empire.
Everything is a blur to me now.
Stumbling over chairs, I can't see in front of me.
The lady of the house never lived here
And all the hearths have gone cold
And I sit wrapped in a shawl of my sadness
And think of the lies that we told.

"I can't see you,"
I say.
"I won't look for you again,"
I say.
"Everything is a blur to me now."

And I grow old.

crying in bars with you

I can't stop crying in bars with you.
We've been doing it since we met,
Since our souls met
swirling as one, our faces wet
with tears from crying in bars with you.

And sure the gin helped a bit,
But I'm so glad my soul gets to spin 'round the wheel with you.
The cosmic chance of it all
that I was born in this age and of this age
to be in love with you.

We cry in bars together, because we both know what's true.
Whatever happens, if the world explodes tomorrow,
my soul is for you.

We should probably pay the bill and get out of here.
Before everyone drowns.

the girl in all the songs

"That song is about you," I mumble.
I'm singing my songs in bed again.
It is as much performative, as it is personal.
My little non-wife turns over,
Her beautiful girl body making mountains in the sheets.
"Is it?"
She asks,
Knowing I wrote the song many moons ago,
Before we met.
"They are all about you, past, present, and future."
You're the girl from the song, honey bunny,
Short and long.
You're the girl in the songs, little lovely.
All songs.

ugly

This is the trend where the guy in the flowy shirt reads poetry
    to you,
except it's not pretty.
It's actually very ugly, and almost hard to look at,
let alone to love.

It's not *for* women,
not on purpose, anyway,
meaning it doesn't pander to women with soft vulnerabilities
that are presented as "tough to admit"
but that in reality are quite digestible.

This vulnerability is acid.
It is molten vitriol, hot on his tongue,
barely making it past his teeth,
and again,
it is very ugly.

Vulnerability in art is so often only as vulnerable as it can be
    while still being lovable.
This is especially true in poetry.
This type of low work,
concerned mostly, it seems, with how the writer has "been hurt"
is not vulnerability.
Neither is it really poetry.

It is blame
of others and of circumstance.
True vulnerability is self-blame.

So, in the spirit of that,
I am manipulative,
I am petty,
I am quick to anger
and short on responsibility.
I am thoughtless,
careless,
and crass.
I have a pathological desire to be right.
I am biting
and go for the jugular.
I am not patient,
brave,
or at times even kind.

I am ugly
but I am trying.

teeth grinder*

It sounds like the stone of an olive cracking between my teeth,
The strong jaw of a worrier. A grinder. A burier.
Botox in your masseters to freeze the muscles in place.
Face feminization.
People say it's because of a gluten intolerance
And I'm probably celiac from the vaccine.
Which vaccine?
All of them probably.
Worrier. Teeth grinder. Burier.
The gritty feeling of bone powder in your mouth when you
    wake up,
Dry mouth and dry lips,
Crushed eustachian tubes and a low-lying undiagnosed sinus
    infection.
It gives you appalling halitosis,
The inability to rebalance the air pressure in your head,
Constant yawning as a facial tic,
Pulling down on your earlobe to create equilibrium.
An overcompensation of the muscles in your throat that step in
    for your weakening masticators.
Which, with time, will permanently alter the look of your face.

Worrier, teeth grinder, burier.

* I worry what this poem is about.

room service

Once I get up to my hotel room I doubt I'll come back down again.
I should have a cigarette.
Fuck it,
I don't need a cigarette.
What I need is a lobotomy
Or some sort of high dose of horse tranquilizer.
It's supposed to be a good day today, weather-wise.
But I still feel like shit.
It's hard to kill yourself on a sunny day.

But then again,
Do more people commit suicide during thunderstorms?
Is there a right time to die?
Why do you "commit" suicide? Or murder?
You don't commit to "dying of natural causes."
You don't commit to living.
Like realism for the delusional,
Like romance for cynics.

"Sir, I'm just checking in to make sure you are checking out?"

I've barricaded myself in my room and unplugged the phone.
It's a hostage situation
With myself as both captor and captive.
I can't commit to a role.
It's harder to commit to cutting my hair
Or taking a job
Or breaking off my engagement
Than to killing myself.

BANG BANG BANG

They are knocking on the door now.
What if they think I am autoerotically asphyxiating myself?
What a horrible fucking way to get discovered.
The internet would have a fun week though.
The postmortem of my body and my life,
The living autopsy of the internet played out upon my death.
What did his tattoos mean?
How big was his dick?
The coroner's report reads like a fucked-up *J-14* quiz.

"Sir? Should I just leave this outside?"
It's room service.
That's who was knocking.
Fuck, I forgot I ordered room service.
Death row food order.
My last meal.
What do you want in your stomach when they cut you open?
I got a cheeseburger, a pizza, and a salad.
Couldn't decide.

I think this poem is done

My biggest fear is ideas incomplete.
It haunts me.
It is the taiko drums that beat in my mind.
Thud thud thud
"You will be without worth."
Thud thud thud
"You will be forgotten."
And of course I will.

No matter how many ideas I complete,
We will, all of us, be forgotten.
My grandfather wore a blue-collared shirt
And he will be forgotten.
He was a failed engineer,
An amateur aviator who only flew a handful of times.
This too haunts me.
He dreamt of flying.
He lived on the ground.
Thud thud thud.
"You will be forgotten."
Thud thud thud.
And of course I will be.

All that's left of him are plastic airplanes
Stained with coffee
And Canadian Club, half drunk.
Half complete.
And so my poems haunt me half complete.
And so my films haunt me half complete.
And so my songs haunt me half complete.

And so my life haunts me half complete.
Thud thud thud
of the taiko drums.
"You will be forgotten, child."
This thud has become my heartbeat.
I have learned to love the drums.

And of course I know I'll be forgotten.

But the things incomplete
Will be done.

the hunter problem

All of my idols were bastards
and drunks
and addicts
and assholes.
I think young men have a problem.

I call it "the Hunter Problem."
As in Thompson,
The only way masculinity allows for sensitivity
is to be suffering from it,
sensitivity.
To be dying of it.
Drinking your feelings into expression.
Expression through aggression.
Art through constant tension.

Young men cling to these people
because even though the world doesn't allow men to be vulnerable
The world allows a drunk to be, or an addict, or an asshole.
It's a way of maintaining your manhood
while exploring the depths of your feelings in public.

As I have gotten older, this matters less to me.
I don't place the same value as I did on this mythologized
    manhood.
This monster. That has maimed and tamed men's expression.
This prison.

I think it's important to mention

My heroes have changed.
The old boozy boys all bore me now.
Show me a Hero who has maintained,
Who has felt all the rage,
And has a wife and kid and a life
And doesn't see their existence as caged.

Show me a Hero who can go the distance.
Show me a Hero who's aged.

more monster

I am sat on my couch,
somewhere between a cigarette, a wank, and a beer
and I'm sad.

My more monster is banging on my ribs
like the bars of some hellish prison.
Nothing pleases him.
There is no fuck, fame, or friend that can quiet him,
only me and my pathetic meditation
and my therapist,
who tells me that some people are born addicts.
Sure, but

how is this not some sickness of modernity?
The peeling paint job of the promise that all your needs are
    acceptable
and that, goddammit,
it's your right
as the customer
to have those needs be met in the quickest way possible.
Why aren't I some monk
or martial arts specialist
made of discipline and morals,
able to eschew Marlboro Smooths, Merlots, and role-play
    sexual dynamics,
able to ignore the hedonistic pleasures of giving in to the most
    base part of myself
and follow faithfully some ancient and divine dogma?

Instead I am on my couch,
somewhere between a cigarette, a wank, and a beer,
and I've just put the coffee on.

the losers' prayer

Having grace when you've won your whole life doesn't
    mean anything.

Patience is only a virtue
when you manage to find it despite being fucked around
    with constantly.
Kindness is a rich person's game.
Every time they say, "I make space to meditate for at least
    an hour every day,"
say a small losers' prayer.

The fortunate have the time to think to themselves,
"How can I show more gratitude?"
"How can I find the strength to be my most present today?"
The strength is found usually in a diverse investment portfolio
and in consciously or unconsciously benefiting from your race,
sexual orientation, gender, or privilege.

It's easy to find grace when you win all the time.
Every time they say, "I've just been very lucky,"
Say a small losers' prayer.

Having grace when you've been grinding it out your whole life?
Now that is something worth measuring.
Never judge a man's character when things are going right.

I think of the people who find the grace to hold the door open
    for someone
after being overworked and underpaid at a job they hate.

I think of the people who, even though their dad just
    recently passed,
have the time to sit and listen to another person's
    personal tragedy.

I think of the people who because of their race, gender,
    orientation, or lack of privilege
suffer the large human indecencies of small passing comments
and yet still find the grace to educate and grow people.

I think of the parents
who find the patience to explain to their children why the sun
    rises and falls.
even though they might lose the house next month.

Grace in the age of winning is easy.
Every time they say,
"You just have to work harder,"
say a small losers' prayer.

pin-up boys

All *Tiger Beat* and *J-14* photo shoots happened in a house in the suburbs of LA where they also sometimes kinda shoot gay porn. You know the posters you had on your walls of all of us? Yeah. Gay porn house.

I just want to say, before all the conspiracy nutjobs jump in, they kept those worlds VERY separate. But it is interesting to note nonetheless. The only reason I found out about it is that I showed up to a shoot on the wrong day. My shoot was for Tuesday. I went there on Monday.

My mum and I drive up to the house that day and are approached by a thin waif of a man, chewing gum. Loudly. "Ummm . . . hi?" he says between chews, pen and clipboard in hand. My mum had come down with me to LA. It was my first or second time there, I think I was like seventeen at the time. She had come, thankfully, to make sure I didn't, you know, immediately get addicted to smack and end up on some casting couch. Good mum.

"We are here for the shoot?" she says brightly. The waif man stops chewing, looks at Mum and then to me and then back to Mum and says, "You . . . Are you sure?" hesitating to say more.

"Not for me! My son. He is getting photographed today. For the magazine." Mum smiles, blissfully unaware. The waif man's face changes. I now recognize what that face was, but at the time I just felt like he didn't like us. His face was one of disgust at my mother. "Wait one second," he says sharply, and goes inside with his clipboard, later returning with a different man, who squints at us from the doorway of the house and waves us in. The waif man calls out from behind him, "Just you, Mom!"

My mother feels like we have done something wrong. She is Canadian and from poverty and terminally feels this way. She felt this way when I did my first audition and the casting director came out into the lobby and called her into the room. She thought I had insulted the very craft of acting in some way and they were going to tell her that I was going to be banned from ever acting again. The casting director instead got me my first agent and put me in my first movie. Mum sighs and gets out of the car and I watch her walk into the house.

Dicks.

She tells me laughing through tears. Just so, so many dicks. Apparently, Mum was called into a makeshift office that had been set up in a guest bedroom, and the walls were covered in pictures of dicks. They were casting for a shoot and were comparing them I guess. They quizzed her on how old I was and why she had brought her son here. Mum explained the mix-up and was sent on her way.

To this day we still laugh about it, but the parallel stands out to me now, one I can't quite place. The pinned-up dicks on the walls, and the posters of me pinned on yours. There is something in there that I can't quite put my finger on.

fame as

Fame as sustenance
Fame as awareness
Fame as a means to a comfortable living situation
Fame as a means of rising up out of the class you were born into
Fame as love
Fame as food
Fame as a free gym membership because you were on TV
Fame as a way of weaving a larger narrative about yourself
Fame as a way of that narrative being taken from you
Fame as a way of turning you into something you aren't
Fame as a gateway drug
Fame as an addiction of self
Fame as the great unequalizer
Fame as a grotesque vulgar mask
Fame as heaven
Fame as acceptance
Fame as finally getting the respect of your peers
Fame as a way for people to talk shit about you
Fame as envy
Fame as a way to separate yourself from the masses
Fame as a way to live forever
Fame as power
Fame as being powerless
Fame as a silly by-product of doing what you are passionate about
Fame as everything that matters
Fame as survivor's guilt
Fame as a tool
Fame as a burden
Fame as a rule

Fame as a hate fuck
Fame as a risk to personal security
Fame as a tired transatlantic flight to London
Fame as endless work
Fame as a way to lose touch with yourself
Fame as the only way to get people to read your book
Fame as a contract you signed without reading the fine print
Fame as the evidence that what you do matters to people
Fame as—

headlines

"The actor best known for _____ has died."
I think it's interesting when an obituary can limit your life
    to a moment.
The teenager best known for throwing up all over the popular
    girl's dress at prom
has sadly passed on,
from embarrassment probably.
The man best known for leaving his kids at the mall once
    by accident
is no longer with us,
having been tragically slain by his wife.

A life reduced to a headline.
So odd.

I've spent my whole life sick at the idea of what my headline
    would read,
Ill with the vanity of that level of self-centeredness,
Nauseated at the idea of being remembered at all,
And furious with the concept of being forgotten,

Worried about dying too early
Or in a boring circumstance
Or in a weird way
That overshadows the things that I made.

Fake immortality.
We don't remember who built Notre-Dame,
Just that it burned.
You will be forgotten,
So why concern yourself with legacy?

Life is like a Japanese Zen garden.
Everything loses shape,
Erodes into sand.

So who gives a flying fuck what you're remembered for?
Me and my silly little self-made markers of success.
Your life isn't the headline.
Maybe your legacy is that your kids liked you,
Or you helped a little old lady across the street,
Or that you planted a garden or whatever the hell you're
    supposed to do
When you are normal and not sick with vanity.
The fucking headline
Screaming out at me
In black and white.

"Ex-teen star dies in industrial meat grinder accident."

curtain call

The fear of faded beauty,
worse than never having had beauty at all.
You fear the falling of your face
before your curtain call.

The nymphettes pointing from beyond the footlights,
cackling with their pretty nubile throats.
Your fear of faded beauty,
flabby necks and feet of crows,

wrinkled hands and crooked nose.
You'll be breathtaking when your beauty goes.

I'm told freedom gives you quite a glow.

tinker bell

She looks up from the mirrored table
and says, "I just like the way the cocaine smells"
She is an actress when she's able
But when she's not, she lives in hell
She lives off you and your fickle love
She doesn't really eat.

I am current
I am valid
I am special
I am new
She screams into the internet
"Big things coming, so stay tuned!"

But she hasn't worked in years
She thought about becoming an influencer
She is addicted to your cheers
And your likes
And your comments
And god *please* subscribe
She released a vegan cookbook once
Just to stay alive

She lives off your attention
And when it fades, she starts to die
She's refused to pursue real happiness
It's probably her pride
It's probably all the things she's kept inside
She most likely needs a therapist
Maybe her content can be like self-help tips online?

That sells, right?
Mental health?
That will stave off her decline
She can partner with a charity
And go to galas all the time

Think of the outfits.

Tinker Bell Tinker Bell
Clap or she'll die.

to the fan who was nice to me

I am on the L train leaving the kingdom of heroin-headed hipsters
and am being carted off to god knows where.
Canarsie
Rockaway
Who knows
It's 3 a.m. and I'm wrapped in my gray coat that covers me
    down to my shoes
I am not sleeping yet
I am dozing
Drifting
Fading in and out of consciousness as the day threatens to break
Drunk with the night and everything in it
And you
In your black boots and box braids
Your soft heavy-lidded eyes and your lip piercing
shake me to keep me from sleep
"Ay. Don't pass out. You'll miss your stop."
I stir for a moment, aware for the first time I wasn't alone
    on the train.
"You don't want to miss your stop."
You are coming home from a punk show,
Some group of screaming anarchists.
Not that I asked,
I can barely form words.
I am coming home from dying
The sort of slow death that takes the clinically depressed, addicts,
    and people with cancer.
"Ay. Don't fall asleep."
My head jerks up.

"What's your stop?"
I mumble something and you nod.
It was obviously clear enough for you to hear it.
"I'll stay with you."
And you did.
And you talked to me about your life and the boy that you like
And I nodded and shook my head with the rocking of the train.
And when we got to my stop you shook me awake.
"This is you."
I stand and stumble toward the train doors as they start to close.
"And by the way, I am a big fan of your work. I grew up with you
    on TV obviously, but I love all the other shit that you do too."
And I fall face first through the open train doors.

slimemouth

"You're like my childhood,"
She says, curling her hair behind her ear with her fingers,
Flirting with me.

Firstly,
If you are trying to fuck me,
making me contemplate my own death by old age isn't
     a great start.
Me internally screaming into the black hole of my own
     existential horror
Is not a hot vibe.

Secondly, I am not "like your childhood."
I was a guy on a show you liked when you were 15.
Your childhood was strip malls,
dry hand jobs,
and jumbo-size Slurpees filled with cheap vodka that dyed your
     tongue bright green.
Slimemouth.

It was your potential not yet attempted
and the arrogance of feeling like you have time on the clock.
You are like 4 years younger than me, by the way.
Keep that in mind if what gets you off is me being old.
Plus.

You are my childhood just as much as I am yours.
I spent my childhood making TV for you to watch
when you had to look after your little brother,
or if school sucked
or if you just wanted to stop growing up for a second.

So really. You are like *my* childhood.
And now I am older,
As you have so kindly pointed out,
And so much happier.
So here is some unsolicited advice from your elder.

Don't idolize your childhood.
Don't succumb to the sedative of nostalgia.
The heroin of yesterday,
Slipping what's left of your life into a warm, numb haze.
Like sliding in the bath with slit wrists.

Make new memories
With people you love.
Move on.
I know the world isn't what you expected it to be.
It hasn't been for me either.
But we must try to build new memories,
To look back on when we are actually old and gray.

Have a new childhood
Again and again.
Every day.

toothpaste affair

I have cut my hair,
I have bought two new suits.
One red and the other blue.
I have bought a pair of aquamarine pin-striped socks
And I am still miserable.

And there she is, standing in our living room, and she hasn't
    noticed
That I have cut my hair
And that I've cut my hand open
and I'm bleeding all over the Moroccan carpets we had shipped.
She is aware of none of this.
She is just standing there.

So I, being as reasonable as I can in this sort of situation,
go to the bathroom and squeeze all the toothpaste down the sink
and grumble,

"I'm going out for toothpaste."

I am wearing one of my new suits,
Either the red one or the blue one, I can't be sure.
I am sure I'm wearing my new aquamarine pin-striped socks.
So I must be wearing the red suit.

I am driving in my powder-blue 1960s Ford Falcon
with dipped blue mags and white walls
down the California streets
and I look fabulous,
as I go to the store to buy toothpaste.

At a stoplight a group of teenagers call out to me from the car
   beside me.
They are all tan-skinned and full of life.

"Are you so and such? I used to watch you on that show when
   I was a teenager!"
So I guess they're in college.

"Alright," I respond.

"I used to want to fuck you." They laugh.

And they drive off
And I go to the store to buy toothpaste.

the sad little fashion boy

I hate being late.
But I hate being underdressed and unnoticed more.

the bull buys a china shop

"You're like a bull in a china shop,"
she says,
"but like if the bull, after breaking all the china, opened
a china shop and was like,
please be careful not to break the china."

So the bull buys a china shop and a shit ton of glue
and tries to glue things back together with you.
But he can't hold the glue stick
because he's all hooves
and apologies.
He's all trauma and horns.

Stomping around all your china.
Doesn't help it's all red,
which to a bull is a trigger.
Actually, it's advertised as "Royal Albert Rose,"
but who cares.
Bullish brute that I am, I can't tell the difference.

But If I'm the bull
then you are the china.

Pretty, but brittle.
How sometimes I wish you had the sturdy unbreakable
quality of '90s IKEA glassware.
You know the ones that were thick blue/green glass?
shaped like a Chihuly sculpture?

Then I could never break you.

So the bull buys a china shop and a shit ton of glue.
and tries to glue things back together with you.

burning yesterday's paintings

I am burning yesterday's paintings,
and I have bits of paper in my pocket of no apparent value
and for no particular reason
I am crying.

I am burning yesterday's paintings because they aren't really all
　　that good.

And I'm told they won't help me paint better, so I am burning them.
At least as firewood and tinder they will give the world more
　　warmth than they had as paintings.

The woman I love is still asleep in my bed, with the *Rosemary's Baby*
　　haircut,
not in the sense that it is demonic, but in the sense that it is
　　quite short.

She will be stirring any minute now
from the smell of burnt canvas and acrylic melting;
she'll most likely rush in and scream,
"Avan, what in the hell are you doing?"

To which I'll respond,
"I'm baking a cake."
And I'll laugh at my joke as she grabs the fire extinguisher.

But that's a hypothetical situation
and I've been told not to dwell on those.

Right now,
presently,
at this exact moment,
I am burning yesterday's paintings.

And I am sort of fine with that.

keloid scar

My skin scarred from where you scratched.
Melanin marked dark
in a shape of half a heart.
Picking at the scab I think,
I'll have it longer than I'll have you.
And I was right.

the religious ecstasy of being in love

since we parted you've started to believe in god.
I don't know if I should take that as an insult.
was god not present in between our breath?
was god not present in our bodies as we discovered each other
up in our tiny bedroom, at the top of the stairs?
I believe that god lived between us,
in our blood and skin,
in your somber eyes, yellow green,
in the long curve of my back,
and, god, in your smile.
yes, god lived within your smile.
you could blow away the world
with just your smile.

(2019)

I wish to give every flower your name.
The fragrant fancy,
Forgotten folly,
Fresh in my nose
And on my tongue.
I wish to know no other flower but by your name.
That every petal would say _____ endlessly
Back at me
As I picked away your thorns.
Oh, to have known your garden only
Holy.
Reborn into fresh daisies
Or roses wrapped in lips of ruby red.

I wish to know no other flower but by your name.
Fields of your flowers,
Your name among plains.

french girl

I've been in Paris looking for that French girl you wanted
    me to be with.
I think your exact words were,
"Sometimes I feel like I am stopping you from being with
    some beautiful Frenchwoman."
You were my beautiful Frenchwoman.
I said it to you every day.
But you never believed me.

Anyway,
I've been sleeping with a girl here.

She's from Santa Barbara.

robert de niro smile lines

One day I will be old and fat and bald
And hopefully happy.
I understand how those old film stars must have felt.
Bathing in cold cream
And warm honey
And the blood of teenagers—
Anything to stave off the inevitable decline of their value
To the machinery of desire

One day I will have smile lines and creases near my eyes.
"Like Robert De Niro,"
My ex-fiancée once told me,
Our relationship, in itself, another marker of time.
Past lovers,
Like so many silly selves,
Sprawled out like desecrated corpses,
Surrounding me,
Useless and dry.
All these skins I have shed.
Skin is the first thing to get older.
Duller maybe,
Colder.
I noticed it first in my hands,
Veiny,
With deeper lines in my knuckles.

I might just need hand cream.

bravery

To be young and brave is no great feat,
For you know nothing
And, in your ignorance,
Know of nothing that can hurt you.

But to be old and brave,
To maneuver around all that fear,
The fear that comes with knowing,
And the type of knowing that comes from having done
And having been hurt.

To navigate those deep waters and to be brave,
To stand full chested at the front of that ship and face those waves,
That is something.

_____ **(1)**

I am lying on my back on the front lawn of a house in the Hollywood Hills. _____'s house is located up some winding long driveway concealed from the world. When your house is that high up, life is all downhill. _____ is very famous. Not like "guy from that show" famous. Like he has transcended into the high-clouded delusion of fame, a fixture in the cultural pantheon of the publicly worshiped, where even the most well-meaning people lose sense of where the ground is beneath their feet.

_____ is well-meaning, but edging, I believe, at times into delusion. For instance, I believe he is freestyle rapping beside me, but I can't be sure, as he is quite bad at it. Yet he bears the confidence of someone who has never been told he is bad at anything in his life. Ever.

We are all high and the sun is now beginning to rise.

I'm 20 and I'm not supposed to be here.

I become aware, very gently, that there are other people sprawled out on the lawn as well. We got here on Friday and I think it might be Sunday morning now. There are girls sprawled all around, in various states of undress. They all seem the same to me. I remember the few conversations I had with them were all about _____, they were all here for the same thing. To be around _____. Some of the girls offered to have sex with me, which I thought was forward and strange. "You know 'cause you know _____." In some act of self-restraint or maybe just hurt pride at getting a fuck by association, I declined. "I'm all right, I'm just here to observe."

_____'s real friends are all men, they were all in fraternities in college, they like football and "chicks" and "getting fucked up." Hollywood is a fraternity, a boys' club I've never felt comfortable or included in. No chicks allowed in the boys' club. Probably because they were in love with each other, the boys. Some of them were actually romantically in love, I think.

They had me along, like a parlor trick or a pet. They were all older than me. "Piano man!" they used to call me. I'd get real high and hang onto the piano all night and hide. I couldn't even really play piano back then. And I was never any good at fitting in. I'd pick a guy and be that for the night. A guise. Just to avoid having to be me.

I was never comfortable up in those hills, could never really breathe.

I'm 20 and I'm not supposed to be here.

I notice that _____ has stopped rapping and has gotten real quiet.

"I don't feel like me," he whispers to himself.

You too, huh?

And so we lie on our backs and stare up at the stars.

And I wondered how many people are who they say that they are.

in the hills, no one can hear you scream

There's always someone doing construction on their
    home in the hills.
I wake up to the chatter of jackhammers and the roar
    of forklifts.
This is Hollywood, everyone is always self-improving.
You can always make something better.
You can always make something more "you."
Rip out the 1920s bathroom
and put in an AI-assisted shower with a sunroof.
You can always update and improve.

I live here too, in the hills.
That's something I'll never get used to.
I grew up in government housing and when I first got to LA
I lived in a trailer in the valley behind some guy's house.
He was a hoarder, so trash was everywhere.
To get home I'd climb over piles of scrap metal
and busted bathtubs
and bags full of empty cheap wine bottles.
Here in the hills, there is no trash.
Armies of maids march up the hill every morning
and march back down again when the sun sets,
carrying garbage bags full of "for your consideration"
    DVD screeners
they used to send to Academy members,
so they know who to vote for come awards season.
In the hills, nothing gets dirty,
at least not on the outside.

Also there's the alarms.
That's something no one tells you when you live in the hills.
When you finally make it to the top, the alarms never stop ringing.
Some rich guy's assistant who can't remember the door code.
It's not her fault, she's being worked to death.
That or someone has broken into the house next door
and brutally murdered the whole family that lives there.
It doesn't even matter.
I am not going to go check.
No one checks in on each other in the hills.
Alarms blaring for no one.
In the hills, no one can hear you scream.
Sharon Tate springs to mind,
sprawled out dead on her marble floor.
Your neighbors aren't checking in on you.

The alarms and the sound of renovations stop only if the
    gardeners are here.
With their leaf blowers and hedge trimmers.
Every house in the neighborhood has their own gardeners.
A community of individuals.
A gardener for every American.
Their schedule is easy to understand.

Monday between 7 and 10, then back again at 12 and 2.
Tuesdays they don't start till 9 but then come back again every
    hour until sundown.
Wednesday it's better to assume they're just going to be there
    all day.
And Thursday–Saturday it's mostly in the morning.
Except for the times that it's in the evenings.

Sunday, obviously, they aren't here,
because that's when the pool guys come.

the last supper

I had to leave LA,
the spray of crazy
and luxury sweatpants.
I had to leave LA,
the boys with their black-faced Rolexes,
their Teslas
and Dries Van Noten bomber jackets.
The always-32 crowd,
hunting and stalking the next crop
of 18-year-old Midwestern models.

I had to leave LA,
some mangled starlet in a cocktail dress
glued to the step and repeat.
"I exist, I exist, I exist,"
she cries desperately into a vodka soda lime.
Lime, not lemon.
Less calories.

I had to leave LA,
the "fraud artist."
Daddy is a partner at a big agency
and his friend owns the gallery.
Got a studio downtown—
you know, sketchy downtown—
'cause he can afford to take risks with his daddy's money.
'Cause he can *choose* to be broke and struggle.

I had to leave LA.
'cause if I stay here any longer,
they will find a place for me.
Eventually they find a place for you.
Some sinner's seat at that sick table.
The last supper.

LA is everywhere now,
pouring out of the telephone,
shining out of a screen.
I thought I could leave LA.
LA lives in my pocket now.

prayer for a pop star

Prayer for a pop star
Blessed is the tweet
Make sure to say the right thing.
Prayers for the meek
Implicate the wicked
Absolve the masses of their sins.
Prayer for a pop star
Go on live to make amends.

Prayer for the actor
Holy is the statement
Beg forgiveness for racist comments made
Movie franchise reinstatement.
Blessed is the press conference
Sacred is the spin
Clemency for atrocities
So that he can act again.

the american wet teen dream machine

She is the ingénue
and she looks like *insert current pop star*

or any of the other "girls next door" that we have sexualized
    and destroyed.
She looks out at us from a magazine, just 18, doe-faced;
    she is licking her lips
and somehow smiling like an angel.

She's America's Sweetheart.
And she looks like *insert current actress.*

She attends a premiere in kitten heels and in a dress that is
    elegant and long
but at the same time altogether "too short"
next to a man three times her age, her leading man,
and she, his following girl.

She is the damsel in distress
and she looks like *insert current pop star.*

She is a brunette and *that's* what makes her interesting.
She has fair-colored eyes
and the most perfect perky breasts you have never seen,
    because that's all part of it.
In an opera or musical she is sung by a lyrical soprano
and she is Juliette.

And you, you Romeo, you romantic, you think,
"I bet you she knows how to cook."
"I bet you she sucks dick like an industrial vacuum cleaner."

"I bet you she could cradle my head while I cry without
    emasculating me."
You romantic, you.
And I bet your mother would *love* her, all the while being
    a tiny bit jealous of her youth.

Because she, like you, has been programmed to value youth
    as a currency
to acquire and to lose.
And the older you get the less value you have
till all you can play is the mother,
whether on-screen or in life.

She is the American wet teen dream machine.
Insert every girl.

silent prayer for the girls of la

The sex object on a billboard
Spread eagle
Blood eagle
Rib cage pulled back behind her spine
Someone's daughter on a billboard
Something like a shrine
The sort of girl you'd get a beer with
The one that lingers in your mind
Someone kind

A girl to claim and say, "She's mine"
Sell the girls off
Each one of them divine
Holy worship of the whoredom
The butcher ties her toes with twine
Silent prayer for the girls of LA
Sell the girls off they'll be fine

what I hear when everything is quiet

McDonald's and a bottle of cheap red wine

Rotten pineapple juice in a piña colada

Fingernail clippings down the side of your dead grandfather's
old couch

The sticky, syrupy stench of cocktail cherries

A Groupon for gender affirmation surgery

Stale beer on a love seat

A white guy's dreadlock in a bottle of Red Stripe

Smoking in front of the hospital

Consensual death

Seafood on an airplane

"We have started our descent" into vulgarity, smut, horror, and
madness. "Please remain in your seat."

Holy water and ice-cold communion wine

It's a Riesling.

Surrealism and champagne

A bottle of brut and sadomasochism

A glass of cava and Caravaggio

The violent, bright paintings of the brutal hangings of the women
who cheated on their husbands with Satan

A discount code for a day spa

Crack cocaine

The call of the last male bird of an endangered species looking
for a mate

I wouldn't fuck you if you were the last avian on earth.

I wouldn't propagate the human race if it meant copulating
with you.

A cigarette and a hand job

A cigar and shibari

Eye contact with an attractive stranger in an airport
Living under the shadow of your father's success
Living in the light of a healthy relationship with your mother
Death at a young age
Death at an old age
Being preserved like pickled herring on life support
A coma and salted caramels
A vegetative state and licorice allsorts
The hard candies old ladies keep in their purses
Amputees fucking on a sex swing
The loss of innocence
The acquisition of curiosity
The acquisition of a holding company
A tax shelter in Panama
Foot fungus in an open-toed shoe
The tiny hairline fractures in your knees due to bending under
    the weight of the servitude of your pointless silly life
An Albertsons reward membership
The hot hatred on the breath of a racist
The dumb, criminal deception of the lies spread on the
    nightly news.
The exhausting and unending drone from the mouth of a leftist
Being morally correct but joyless and boring
The death of nuance
The birth of digestible information for the masses
Lumps or soft masses near or around your lymph nodes that
    are not cancer they don't think but they can't be sure unless
    they do a biopsy
A familiarity with the cold embrace of death
A comfortability with violence that most people spend their whole
    lives avoiding
Mike Tyson biting Evander Holyfield's ear

Achilles putting his shoes on very carefully
The knowledge that everyone you know will die
The quiet admission of apathy at the death of strangers
A girl in yoga pants
Piety in the face of heresy
Hypocrisy in the face of moral absolution
Hard-core pornography that makes you question your
    feminist values
Hate-watching *The Bachelor*
The throbbing or thrumming of your prick or cunt at the
    thought of copulation
A Terry's chocolate orange
A Flair Airlines flight home for Christmas
A miscarriage
The green jealousy of betrayal
The red anger of an offense to your ego
The silly worry that your partner is more sexually experienced
    than you
The sorrow of seeing a bygone lover
Believing but not knowing that the universe has a plan for you
Holding onto grudges because they are comfortable
The horrible feeling of people talking behind your back
A sexual experience with a family member
Wrestling
Space, the final frontier
Esoteric cultural practices
The dying bleating of a sheep killed for religious rites
UN ratifying a vote to condemn mass atrocities
Rescinding that vote in favor of the Industrial War Machine
Heart-shaped lockets
Obstruction of justice and a tart Chianti
Makeup sex

Breakup sex
A healthy nonsexual relationship with a person of the
    opposite sex
Chick-fil-A and ketamine—

nirvana is just subspace

She isn't a yoga teacher,
She is a dominatrix.
"Get the strap and place it between your legs. Put your blocks
    behind you and bend back onto them."
This is yin yoga. Allegedly.
The kind of people who become yoga instructors are interesting.
Imagine being so intense that you HAVE to become calm
and then having found your calm,
A practice that quiets the 1,000-mph hell storm that is your inner
    psyche.
You decide, "I wish to impose this practice upon the world
    and control the bodies of the inferior, the weak, and the
    unconverted."
Pretty fucked-up shit, you psycho.
She is marching around behind me,
stomping like a cop,
adjusting the bodies of the lesser.
Not very chill vinyasa go-with-the-flow girl of you, Julie.
The most intense people become yoga instructors,
'cause they have to or they'll explode.
They need control.
True top/dom behavior.
But they don't want to come across as someone who needs
    to be in control.
They want to be the fun girl,
the go-with-the-flow girl.
But really they want to twist you into a pretzel and step on
    your back
or control your breathing.

Sicko.
Maybe that's why I resist yoga class.
There can't be two perverts trying to run the show.
Nirvana is just subspace
and I'm not gonna get topped by a white girl with a namaste
    tattoo.

leather bondage (in vegan leather)

"The vampire gloves with the spikes only come in vegan leather,
as does the bullwhip and the mouth gag."
"That rope is made of a biodegradable hemp composite;
    actually, it has a lot more give than jute, but it's better for
    the environment."
Even our sex toys are environmentally conscious.
Sometimes you just want to bind someone down with play-safe
    tape that won't fall apart given a little resistance.
How much pleasure are you willing to give up to save the planet?
Maybe you just want a straw that fucking works.
Oil spills off the Gulf of Mexico,
but I can't get a paddle that doesn't fucking break on me.
"Carbon footprint" was press spin from oil companies to
    make us all feel personally responsible for them ruining
    the fucking planet.
Companies don't have footprints. We do.
How many paper bags have broken?
How many smashed eggs?
Why is this my responsibility? Should there not be a regulatory
    body that *makes* manufacturers use biodegradable shit?
"We're all in this together."
I guess we should *try* and make changes,
feel personally guilty,
all the while knowing who is to blame.
Whatever.
I'm just trying to find a high-quality flogger.
How much pleasure are you willing to give up to save the planet?

**don't just skip to this poem,
read the others first**

In praise of whores.
If this isn't you, read on.

messy sticky little truths

Spilling across your stomach
Like fresh goat's milk
Breast golden brown
And auburn ribbons
Tied down
Soft-smelling
Full of fucking and sadness
Filled with thrusting and trust
Messy, sticky little truths
I pour over you
Writing on you in spit
Sentences said without speaking
You've tasted all I have to say
Inside you

dog treats

She was bored and full of fucking.
And I had a pocket full of dog treats.
I was sniffing around.
What are you doing?
You and your replacement companion.
Dog meat.
Look at him, all up on his hind legs.
Good boy.
I know you're bored.
And full of fucking.
And I have my pocket full of dog treats.
And you've trained him up real nice.
All up in his hind legs.
At dinner parties.
So well-behaved when he meets your mother,
he doesn't jump up at all.
He's gotten even cuter
since he was neutered.
But I know you're bored
and full of fucking
and I have my pocket full of dog treats.

sour sweat

Your sweat tastes sour
Caked to your neck
Regret
And other feelings of worthlessness
Another hotel room
With your braids wrapped around my forearm
Bleach blond
Brown skin
Wet
Swallow hard
Hypomania and sex
What feels good to you one week
Feels shameful the next
Sour sweat

_____ **(2)**

_____ **has invited me over** to her house. I'm a kid. It is 4 a.m., and I have to film The Show the next day. I shouldn't go, but I have a curious nature. My curiosity is what kept me up most nights back then, too interested in "finding out" to go to sleep. These days I am in bed pretty early—lost my curiosity, I guess. Or at least I'm less curious about what goes on in famous girls' bedrooms at 4 a.m. I jump into my powder-blue 1966 Ford Falcon, light a filter-less Lucky Strike cigarette, and start the engine. I am a ridiculous individual. I am a performer. An explorer. A detective. *Camp* I believe is the term used. But I have always been an investigator first, even before being an actor, and tonight, I'm too curious to sleep.

The house is situated in a fancy suburb of Los Angeles. It's not exactly Mulholland Drive fancy; it's fancy if you were born out of the mud and quickly became famous and rich. The kind of fancy the truly rich look down on. So to me, it was very fancy. I mean, they have a fucking security gate. Security buzzes the gate open, and I drive up the winding long driveway. The guard is standing in front of the house. He nods at me in a particular way, the nod of someone who is hired to not say anything and yet the kind of nod that says something without saying it. An imperceptible smile. A smirk. That they are letting some kid blowing smoke out of a powder-blue 1966 Ford Falcon into their boss's house at four in the morning. They like to see her have a good time I guess. I think mostly they like to gossip.

_____ is dressed for bed, but also dressed as if she is pretending to go to bed but instead is sneaking someone into her house. So cute, but cozy. As I park the car, she waves at me from a balcony off to the side of the house above an eight-car garage. _____ has glitter all over her face, and wild, intense eyes. She is chewing on something I can't quite make out and waving furiously. "Come on!"

Everyone in the house is asleep, _____ assures me. "Everyone" meaning her mother, her sister, her brother, and an assortment of staff I never end up meeting. _____ lets me in through the balcony off of her bedroom so I don't see the rest of the house, but the room has that *MTV Cribs* rented-furniture vibe to it. Like if you were very wealthy in a suburb of Dallas, Texas. Barely any distinct style or notable personality to it other than the assortment of Starbursts, gummy bears, Twix, and Ring Pops she has covering her bed. Honestly, there is more candy in that room than I've ever seen centralized in one place outside of a gas station. All the lights in the room are switched off except for the illuminating glow of a TV in the corner.

The Nanny is on. I am aware of this because of the sound of Fran Drescher's voice. "I love this show, she is so hot." _____ takes my jacket, which I thought was very traditional and strangely kind of sweet, and she sits me down on her bed and offers me candy after candy. All of which I decline.

I don't have much of a sweet tooth and we fuck a fair few times. Hard to tell the difference between the sounds of sex and Fran Drescher's voice. So no one in the house wakes up.

I decided to have a Ring Pop and we watch *The Nanny* in her bed as she lies on my chest. I had never really seen the show until that night. It's funny, it's good, I liked it. Fran Drescher is very talented. _____ can't sit still for long and is up pacing the room, showing me things. At first she shows me a bag she got from Paris fashion week. "It's nice." I didn't know much about fashion back then. I had style, which is different than knowing what an archival Givenchy clutch looks like. Then she rushes to her computer and pulls up some demos of scratch vocals Michael Jackson did on the song "Bad" that she bought at an estate sale. "Cool." I get the sense she is trying to impress me. I don't know why—she's the famous person.

We fuck again and end up on the floor this time. *The Nanny* has been replaced by a late-night infomercial for hair curlers. _____ gets up and stumbles to the bathroom and I lie there naked, looking up at the ceiling. I check my watch. Seven a.m. I have to be at work in an hour. A Ring Pop is in my mouth. I get up as _____ returns from the bathroom. She has even more glitter on her face now for some reason. I tell her I have to go to work and climb down the balcony as the sun is rising. Security smirking. I get into my car.

My whole face is covered in glitter. Like I was fucking a fairy. I stick my tongue out in the rearview mirror, my tongue stained blue from the Ring Pop. Luckily, I have an hour of makeup before we actually shoot anything today. So long as I get to set on time. Traffic starts early in Los Angeles. I drive the Falcon down the long winding driveway to the gate that opens slowly. *Ding.* A text.

"Wanna come to my birthday?"

My curious nature.

"Sure."

voyeur

What a fun time
To watch the teen idol fall.
What fun to watch
Their flaws
and their "feelings"
and their fucking.
Purple links on websites of celebrity nudes.
You love to watch,
You voyeur,
You freaky lil' fuck.
You like to watch, don't you?
Maybe the real pervert is you.
At least we are fucking participating in the orgy of the internet,
You and your little mask at the sex club,
As you partake in this nonconsensual masturbation
Of watching us fail.
Freak.
And who are you to watch?
It's not just us naked you want to see.
You want to see our tragedy
And our pain.
You sadist.
You love to watch.
Just wait until it's you.
Just wait until they take your search history and use it against you.
Just wait until they gather up all your sins too.

sex joke during the *J14* interview

Two types of kids get into acting on children's television.
Church kids and tiny little freaks.
Go ahead and guess which one I was.

The church kids are good 'cause they are amazing singers;
     they are great at doing what they are told; and, because
     they learned scripture, they can recite whatever garbage shit
     these shows write for them.

Then there was us. The tiny little freaks.
The advantage we had on the church kids is that we had
     that spark.
You know, the X factor.
The X factor here being early stages of some form of
     mental illness.

We seemed to go one of two ways.
We either get bored and decide we could use our superpowers
     for other more rewarding things,
or we completely implode,
becoming drug-addled messes.
I did the former,
I'd say mostly because I was lucky that my parents weren't fuckups.

It was funny watching the church kids and the tiny little
     freaks interact.
The terse and controlled laughter of a church kid as a tiny
     little freak makes a wildly inappropriate sex joke during
     the *J-14* interview.

Anyway, this is less of a poem and more of an observation.

**you are never going to believe
what this child star looks like now**

"Like if you miss _____!"

Never has a generation regurgitated their own childhood
    so quickly.
As soon as it was swallowed,
thrown up on our shirts.
Like babies who haven't been burped.

"Only '90s kids will get this!"

Is it because we so fear what is to come?
The black throbbing unknown of tomorrow,
its dark tentacles with unseeable and unknowable ends
wrapping themselves around our future.
AI eating everything endlessly,
its gaping maw, wet with all our dreams both broken and
    not yet born,
simulacrum,
until our present is a cheap plastic replica
of a formally important and meaningful concept.
Copy the copy.
Rerelease the franchise.
Out with the new.
Repeat the old.

"Comment if you remember _____!"

How can we not remember what just occurred?
Probably because of the fog of the constant content,
the blurring of days,

a haze of celebrity breakups, TV show finales, and horrific
    tragedies.
Aren't they canceled? And for what? Do we remember?

The dazed look of a beaten fighter before they hit the mat,
unable to make sense of what's hitting us.

"You are never going to BELIEVE what this CHILD STAR
    looks like NOW!"

the angels of suburbia

I'm back in LA
And it's day
And I have my fucking iced latte
And I'm here.

It's been 2 days
But it's also been 12 years.

It's amazing how quickly suburbia sets in.
I have to remember to send her some hard-core pornography
so she is reminded of how we started.
And the sun is shining
And I have a fucking breakfast burrito
And it's good.

"Here, homie,"
As I'm handed some Tapatio.
And it's growing on me again,
The freeways
And the ignoring of the world set ablaze by the drums of war,
And her tiny little Pekingese that keeps jumping up on me.
And it's fine.

I don't know how many 40-year-old single dads
With their hair in a topknot
And girlfriends in their 20s
I can see before I become one.
Telling my son Button to "talk out your feelings, buddy,"
Just to have him grow up into a cokehead club predator.

But I love her
So I'm here
And I know myself.
I like writing poems complaining about suburbia
More than I actually want to leave it.
I am what I believe was once called a "family man."
And it's nice here.

I said that last time too.
But this time is different.
This time she is listening to me.

ny/la

New York can turn you actively crazy,
like riding-the-subway-naked,
eating-your-socks kind of crazy.
Out of your mind, but active.

Los Angeles can turn you a different kind of crazy,
the slow, lazy kind of crazy,
the morally numb kind of crazy
that makes you okay with all manner of abject inhuman indecencies.

Either way, you're going crazy.

love has a number

"True love is for the wealthy. I have to find someone to split bills
    with. Someone to rent with, get on each other's health plan,
    whoever has the best coverage."

Love has a number,
Especially in New York.
Couples copulate to the sound of bank transfers.
I pay internet,
You pay utilities,
And we all end up like whores.
Love has a number,
3,800 a month
19' apiece.
He gets most of the dinners
In order to keep up gender appearances
But she pays for the groceries.
Postmates they split
But he gets the Ubers.
They sometimes take trips
But she has to work on her computer all weekend.
Overtime pays too good.
Love has a number.

playing in traffic

It's safer to walk toward traffic, no matter how fast it's going.
To face your problems head-on.
Because if you walk on the other side of the street,
you'll get struck dead and never even know what hit you.
I feel this same way about love.
It's not easy, you know, to walk toward the traffic,
but I'd rather our love was struck dead by the truth we could see
than never knowing what hit us.

artist in residence

I feel like the custodian of the museum of her feelings.
Don't touch the ancient Chinese jars of her past trauma!
They are very rare and easily breakable.
Except they aren't really all that rare these days.

I stay until I become her museum's curator.
I choose the exhibits now.
Help her organize them by era.
The lithographs of her "best friends that betrayed her,"
the ancient Mesopotamian tapestries of "toxic ex-boyfriends,"
the prehistoric early cave paintings of "father trauma,"

till we get to the contemporary exhibits,

where I am no longer curator but creator.
Hell, I'm the artist-in-residence,
making new pieces every week.
New works for you to collapse into a torrent of sadness over,
to hang on your walls when I'm gone.
I wonder how you will display me when I'm history.
Will I be some brutal foreign empire that leveled your cities?
Some proud and forgotten people you look back at with
    admiration?
What will I mean to you in your personal museum,
where all of history relates to you?

Sometimes sadness is a kind of narcissism.

the great schism

The iconoclasm of our love.
When it was over,
It was like a great library burning down.
Alexandria
Alexandria
Alexandria
It almost sounds like your name.
Gone are the tomes and tapestries of all that was us.
Our jokes,
our fights,
our sex,
our art.
All burnt.
The great schism of our love.
The great schism of the heart.

the cult of the moon and of soft bodies

I've spent so many winters
writing love letters to historical figures.
The women of wars and woes,
goddesses of myth
Infanta Maria
and Yaa Asantewaa
and the golden stools on which they sit.
My darling Gentileschi,
with the beheading blade
of brush and paint.
Artemisia, who slayed her Assyrian aggressor.
Where are all those huntresses of Artemis?
Mine is a cult of the moon and of soft bodies.
But why, when I came to you,
did I treat you as a mortal?

are you well?

Cast by the gods
but cast down by mortals.
Pools of endless water,
portals.
Will I see you again
when I see you again
or will I see someone I've never met?
Will I see a back to which my hand has never rest?
All things conclude and arrive at their end.
Are you well?
I know we're not friends.

Did I change everything?
Tin rings bent before they break
and more romantic gestures.
Just my little truths that I slip under you.
I press my tongue into the bruises of your fruit.
Nectar wet nectar wet.

Cast by the gods
but cast down by mortals
Pools of endless water,
portals.
Will I see you again
when I see you again
or will I see someone I've never met?
Will I see a back to which my hand has never rest?
All things conclude and arrive at their end
Are you well?
I know we're not friends.

46 weeks

Baby, take it easy on me. Please.
Move on slowly for me.
I swear it isn't greed,
it isn't greed.
Maybe
it's a need to know that sometimes you still think about me.
So maybe I concede
that it's selfish
but I swear it isn't greed,
it isn't greed.

You've been
tearing our temple down brick by brick
to make it less painful for you.
I admit, I've tried,
but I couldn't bear to see you that way.
I've always seen you as kind.

I always seem to defend you in my mind.

I briefly forgot the color of our sheets.
It's hasn't been that long—
45 weeks.
The sheets were army green.
Not the color green that we ordered,
but we are far too busy and distracted to change them.
And that seemed to be the theme:
far too busy and distracted to change it.

And maybe just too weak.
46 weeks.

poor little pop star girl

My lonely wife calls me on the phone
From empty hotel rooms in Paris Denver New York and then Rome.
And she is hardly ever home.
Poor thing.
Poor wife.
Poor little pop star girl.
Go.
Get out there, little girl.
This is what you've waited for
When you were all poor and alone.
This is what feminism is for, I'm told:
A debilitating job that makes you feel guilty.
Working yourself to the bone,
Bound by your work.
You wanted to be a big girl.
Now look how you've grown.

cultural coprophagy

There are no new cities.
No new towns
Just regurgitated buildings
And traffic and sound
No new culture.
No new discovered place,
Nothing found.
Like a dog,
Throwing up to eat our own sick.
Like a dog,
Round and round.
Cultural coprophagy.
No new art.
No new films.
No new books.
No new poems.
Not that there ever was,
But we have been eating our own shit for so long now,
We've sucked all the nutrients out.
Nothing new, baby
Till it burns to the ground.

hypochondriac

I've been back in LA for half a day
and someone has already handed me a Zicam nasal spray.

It's impossible to not become a hypochondriac here
with all these insane people,
workaholics who can't get sick.
California is not the "lay back, go with the flow" state it claims
    to be.
It is sick with people paranoid of being ill
because it means they can't work.

It's so easy to develop a "thing" here.
The gluten-free, paraffin-free, vegan, raw, nontoxic, plastic-free,
antibiotic, chemical, cancer-causing chaos
that is trying to pick out a fucking organic shake.
They all want to live forever.

Personally, I ate McDonald's for most of my childhood and
    my chance of dodging colon cancer is as good as any other
    poor person.

Why do you want to live forever? To watch LA burn to a crisp?
To bear witness to the fall of humanity?
I am too used to food being delivered to my doorstep
To be prepared to flee from the rape bandits during the end times.

I don't know, man.
I don't know if I'm trying to last that long.

the transamerica junkie relocation program

"We got to move them out!"
Sure they do.
How are they supposed to raise the rent
with all these junkies about?
Like Memphis Mike with Sharpie all over his face
so he looks like Batman.
I was drunk once and let him up to my apartment.
He said he could play the piano,
and so I let him and he could, although not very well.

And the tin cans are worth a penny.

"We must make our neighborhoods safe!"
Sure, of course you must.
How are they supposed to attract young trust fund couples
    to the area
without first making it safe enough for Starbucks and
    Restoration Hardware to move in and sell them things.

In fact, Yolanda Graves does her makeup in a Starbucks
    bathroom mirror every morning.
The staff are actually pretty nice about it,
so long as she doesn't drag her johns into the john
and she leaves as soon as the office crowd arrives.
And she wears cheetah heels
and cherry lipstick
and she wasn't born in her own body.

And the plastic bottles are worth 5 cents.

"We must protect our children!"
And sure why not,
as long as they aren't born into poverty,
forced into public schools that fail them, and thrown into jail,
because then they are not children, they're bad eggs.

Like Ziggy, a neighborhood kid: his dad is dead and his mom's
    a drunk
and he is huffing air-conditioning coolant out of a plastic bag
    in the park
and smashing rocks through schoolyard windows
and getting arrested in strip mall parking lots.

And he is happy his dad is dead
and sad his mother drinks
and he wishes he could do better in school
but he can't.

And wine bottles are worth a dime.
but Ziggy knows that all too well.

the landlord buys a sand castle

The son of an investment banker plays in the sand by the ocean.
He is building a sand castle,
but also a highway, a commercial/residential living space,
    and a car park.
I watch him work,
digging his hole,
working harder than he will ever work in his life.
I watch him dig
hand over fist
digging up muddy sand
and oil
and gold
and cobalt.
I see him work with his hands for the last time in his life.
Before they are used to send emails,
file lawsuits,
evict tenants.
And he keeps on digging 'cause he can't stop.
He might dig his way through the earth in his need for more
    muddy sand
to build housing tenements, shipping yards, and office buildings.
I watch him work harder than he will ever work in his life
and then
when the water comes
and washes away his greedy city of sand
I'll watch him lose for the first time.

a group for every outsider

When did our rebels get so safe?
We all have our own little words now,
everything is so well-defined.
We used to be voluptuous, unknowable, and vague,
and now look at all our values!
The promise of a group for every outsider.
No one is alone!
A car for every American!
We all get a marriage and loan!
When did our rebels get so safe?

Where is the fuck and the filth
when everything is so well-defined?
If they name us then they can sell to us
so we started naming ourselves
to make it easier for them.
What a fun little ride!
A group for every outsider.
No one left behind.

that guy used to be someone

A group home for aging artists.
I can't remember shit, but fucking who cares.
Not you and your documentary team and your stupid fucking
    makeup assistant.
I am in my own perverse gallery now, hung up,
beds upon beds, all lined up for you.
A group home for aging artists.
You loved me when I was young and full of fuck and vinegar.
I loved me then too,
but do you love my aging, rotting body,
my mind a mess of paint and noise?
Imagine you
treating me as a baby with a shit-filled diaper.
And sure, my diaper is full of shit.
But at least my heart isn't,
and yours will always be.

My soul has been filled with diamonds and uranium.
Yours are filled with the contents of my fucking diaper.
The only advantage you hold over me, son, is your fucking youth,
and you will lose that too.
A group home for aging artists all filled with versions of you.

doing business in the dark

There is a serial pooper defecating in the aisles of the theaters
    on Broadway,
doing his dirty business in the dark,
only to be revealed between acts,
when the house lights are on.
He shat next to Hillary Clinton once.
During Hamilton.
I heard he was arrested with his pants down.
We are the same,
me and this dirty little defecator.
We like to do our business in the dark.
We like to do what we are told not to
for art
or in protest.

blood tastes like metal

Blood tastes of metal. This is well documented. But what people talk about less is that it's also sort of sweet.

Rachael Ray is playing on the tv attached to the ceiling and Amelia, the dental hygienist, is scraping away large chunks of my plaque-plagued gums.

Blood tastes of metal but it's also sort of sweet.

Rachael has some quack on the show who is rambling on about the berries from a hidden Bolivian valley that reverses the growth of cancer cells and gives you perfect skin and repairs your broken relationship with your father.
I'm at the point where I'm hopeless enough to believe him.

I have decided to no longer live in the world of fact, but rather I wish to inhabit the fantasy of early-morning talk show remedies and late-night infomercials that sell you knives sharp enough to cut through the general malaise of having been born.

Only $9.99 for the set.

Amelia is now drilling. I believe if she continues in this manner, she'll strike oil.
Blood tastes of metal but it's also sort of sweet.

"Do you floss?"

Ah, this part.

The part where I obviously lie and say "yeah." Knowing full well that she is staring at evidence to the contrary. "Well I was, but I haven't in a few weeks," I meekly add, an attempt to give legitimacy to this embarrassing facade. She accepts my blatant deception like a trained professional and continues her barbaric torture of my bleeding gums.

"Well you should, *floss is boss*."

She has said this before, in fact I think she says it every time. I can't be the only person in here bullshitting about my ability to care for myself. We are all of us just merely trying. Attempting to seem as together and on top of it as all the açai-berry-eating, low-fat, low-carb, low-self-esteem rise-and-grinders that we see in magazines or Instagram or *Rachael Ray*.

Rachael has moved on to a story about some woman who hasn't seen her twin sister in 13 years or misplaced her cat, or something like that. "More from Sherlyn after the break." They go to commercial. The County Hospice Lotto is giving away a 1.7-million-dollar megamansion you can die in as Amelia's face mask is splattered with blood.
Blood tastes of metal but it's also sort of sweet.

"Suck."

She says it firmly. Her tone steady and authoritative. I obey as the pinky spit pooling in my mouth is hoovered away.

At what point do you start to listen blindly to your captors? I wonder as Amelia gets the floss and begins doing what I said I've been doing, sort of, kind of, sometimes.

Sherlyn and Rachael are back; this time they are cooking.
Sherlyn is explaining her family's secret soufflé recipe. Nine generations of French farmers who, legend has it, got the recipe from the chambermaid of Marie-Antoine Carême, the famous Parisian souffleér. It's amazing what you'll give away for free if they stick a camera on you. Selling your secrets to swine for a 15-second spot on TV and a *Rachael Ray* swag bag.

It's amazing what you'll let your captors do.

"Spit,"

Amelia says.

smile, strange and strained.

I am trying to remember when I started smiling so tightly.
The creases round my mouth strange and strained
Eyes squinting, obscuring my sight.
I try to recollect exactly when it changed
From the free and wild smile of my youth
To something more contained
To something careful and considered
To something more arranged
To something I don't recognize
To something more deranged
I am trying to remember exactly when it changed
Back when my smile was unrestrained.
The skin tight across my face now
All tense, unnatural, and trained.
I worry it is not joy lost
But something sad that I have gained
Some sad new smile that's here to stay
A smile that's tightened up my face.

conversations through the walls

If you listen long enough to conversations through the walls,
the laughing starts to sound like crying
and the crying starts to sound like laughing
and the truth you can't hear at all.

The couple next door to you are dying
and maybe they were better off as friends
and when they stop their fighting to make love
you listen to them speak with hating heated breaths.
Hot and heavy "I hate you's"
between orgasms, marriage, kids, and death.

If you listen long enough to the conversations
that whisper between the walls,
the loving starts to sound like lying,
the lying starts to sound like loving,
and their whispers you can't even hear at all.

swinging for the fences

I really closed my eyes and swung the bat,
falling in love with you.
I decided from the first day we met that you were it for me
and if I couldn't make it work with you
then it'd just be me,
forever,
wandering the world a lone soul,
and that I'd be fine.

Of course, now I know that I wouldn't be.
'Cause it's just me now,
having swung the bat blind
and missed
and I've never felt more alone.
Whoever said, "It's better to have loved and lost than to have
    never loved at all,"
is a fucking moron.

I don't know, maybe they are right.
Maybe I'll never regret swinging.
How lucky we were, I guess,
to find something worth swinging for the fences.

scene partner

None of the women I've ever dated knew my favorite flower
Or even asked.
I knew theirs.
Calla lilies
Sunflowers
Roses
And foxgloves.
I think much is made of love.
The performance of it.

But like a really good actor
I am not lying or pretending.
I am telling my truth
With full voice,
So that the people sitting in the last row can hear me

I fight through all the same embarrassment that they do
And shame
And fear
And worthlessness
To step up on the stage
To show up unafraid
And show them that I love them.
Never had a scene partner that really felt the same—

That or they had stage fright.

So I know your favorite flower
And what you like to eat from your favorite restaurant.
And I will go pick up that thing
And remember that fact.

But I've never had an actor do it back.

magical thinking

my priestess in a nightdress
standing in the window
staring up at her mother's stars.
and sighing,
"to think! there is so much magic out there!"

healers, witches, wild-eyed sprites, and fay

I've only ever been able to fall in love
with healers, witches, wild-eyed sprites, and fay,
whose power lures knights into foggy woods and,
should they will it,
out of those same woods, changed.
I, some gallant horseman,
bent by threads of fate,
ride up to where the river sways.
Riding for our king and some old chivalric sense of honor
and, of course, for faith.
And for all those foolish matters that concern
men of the crown and women chaste.
I ride up to where the river sways.
through the wood
to those gnarled roots
to your gates.
to your harpies hollow with your sisters.
And there we'd lay
and your sisters would brush my hair
remove my boots
and bid me stay.
And you would heal my wounds
and cleanse my body
and of course, you'd pray.
In some tongue
unfamiliar to my Christian ears,
the words of earth and clay.

Older than the oldest testament
older than the rain.
Lay me down with you and your harpy sisters
until my dying day.
For I've only ever been able to fall in love
with healers, witches, wild-eyed sprites, and fay.

blue nude bruised

Our love is linked to the phases of the moon,
and I know that you were phased
by the changes in my mood.
And often I was sad, but it was never you.

Blue nude bruised
black and blue.

Our love is governed by the wailing of the winds.
And I know you would've liked to be both my lover and my friend
but that would never do.

Blue nude bruised
black and blue.

Our love faltered when it was halted by our age.
I saw your pretty little light go out
when you felt you were betrayed
and I wish it wasn't true.

Blue nude bruised
black and blue.

Our love was ruled by the brightness of the sun.
There are words and gestures made
that can never be undone.
And when our light began to fade
and the evening is begun,
the phases of our love were blinded by the brightness of the sun.

Blue nude bruised
black and blue
and I was bruised by you.

jester

I held court for your feelings
at your side,
as we presided over the many wars and treaties of your heart,
that kingdom of yours that saw so many battles.
And when the troubles of the crown weighed on your mind,
you would turn to me,
your confidant and adviser
and sometimes
your jester,
and I would assure you against some doubt you had
or make you laugh
and privately, away from the eyes of nosy courtiers,
you would let me hold you
firm and full
in the way no one should ever hold a queen
in the way that one would hold a child.
and yet in the only way that ever soothed you

deserving of worship

She said, "Don't enter the temple like a fraud,"
Or like some false god
Pray for the prey
Worship for the weak
I'll eat your heart
You'll love me
You'll love me
I've made you love me
Pray to me
Worship
As a form of bondage
But not for her
She has been waiting in her temple for a prophet
Waiting for feet to wash
Hair covered, copper bowl in hand
Waiting to worship.
I must make myself deserving of it.

I am reminded of the painting
of the creation of adam

She shyly muttered something about the lord
Moved her hand to mine at her own accord
And soared.

God exists between our fingertips and vocal cords
Breaking hands
and voices cracking under the weight of something planed
    and fate ignored
Divine interception,
Holy and bored

The saints of chaos play their lyres
To the sound of liars teething
And just as the breaking of the day
is followed closely by the evening
So does fate chase the crackling spark
that the flames of chance are leaving
god was dancing in our palms that day,
And filled our hands with so much meaning

So it was randomness and chance, they'll say,
that led to all this pain and grieving.

holy pervert

Praying like some holy pervert
Her knees knocking together like church bells.
Prostrate below, like some wild crying believer.
Zealous zealot,
her hands grasped around a rosary
weeping for Christ
weeping for the sins of men
and then finally
weeping for her own sins.
Confession,
the committing of acts depraved and natural to her.
Confession,
and finally forgiveness,
for her Father loves her
and her god would never turn away a whore.

I fight hard, dirty probably

Please don't break on me.
I fight hard, dirty probably.
Please don't break on me.
You were built fragile,
better to say delicately
with all your pretty pieces,
all your moving parts,
and me, your rough man
with my three-piece suit
and three-piece heart.
Your many fragments are illusive to me
as I bash around
looking for what I need.
Please don't break on me.
I fight hard,
dirty probably,
but what beauty in a heart intricately built,
rather than mine, clumsy and crass.
Please don't break on me,
pretty little heart made of glass.

in the morning.

I wake up in horror and anticipation
and my stomach aches
and it's because of the coffee
and the million other things
that in the morning call upon my heart to break.

Every morning I am born into a new day
like a newborn baby,
helpless, lonely, and afraid.
In horror and anticipation
and coffee is my mother
and the coffee makes my stomach ache.

And it's the million other things
that in the morning
call upon my heart to break.

I am born into the morning.
Out of darkness nothing I awake
and maybe yesterday happened
and maybe today will be different
and cigarettes are my father
and they make my stomach ache.

And I should probably eat something.

And it's the million always things
that in the morning
call upon my heart to break.

the santa ana fires

I awoke from a nightmare, in a cold, wet sweat
to the burning of the Santa Ana fires.
I was shaking and hysterical.
And you held me as I cried myself to sleep.
And then we awoke into ash.

Dabbled daylight through the smoke.
I smoked outside in the summer's winter storm and wrote.
Ash like falling snow.
And then we went to breakfast.

We had coffee next to a 6-foot-4, blond-haired teenager with
    bandages on her nose.
She was so tall I could barely see her face through the clouds
    of gray.
And I wondered if she could see me watching her.
and if she did, she looked away
and then we drove.

Through the hills and valleys in the fog of fire's cloak,
the streets so vertical you fear you're falling.
We drove until we reached the coast
and then we stopped and spoke.

Laughing, telling jokes,
watching birds fly low in order not to choke.
The fire raged and raged through the hills until it had eaten up
    half the coast
and then we made a boat.

And sailed as far west as you can go,
watching, as behind us, the world we knew went up in smoke.
And I looked into your eyes and smiled,
the smell of salt and rigging rope.

For I knew the Santa Ana fires had burned my fear and
    left me hope.

ode to patti smith

"I gotta go," Patti sighed
"I gotta wash my old man's clothes"
Daddy-o got to get clean
And go go go.
Feminism means a clean set of clothes.
Ironed shirt, tie, and a pair of trousers.
Pleats all neat for your daddy-o.

Even Patti Smith ironed clothes.
The hands of a poet
Bound in yellow rubber washing-up gloves.
Imagine wasting those
Fingertips meant for writing prose.
Not that there's shame in the domestic game
But that's not Patti's bag, daddy-o.

Good god, you look good in my suit.
In that fuck-me haircut,
All short and cute.
Patti Patti you lovely bitch wolf queen,
Don't go.
Don't go become the poet mother
Stay here and clean clothes.

heavy lidded eyes for crying

Arty white boys want to love her.
She is like hot bathwater.
And lavender.
She cools quickly
And smells sweet.
And her friends keep on dying
So she stays in the bath and weeps as she reads.
Thank god the arty white boys want to love her.
She uses them to fill needs.
Sex never really felt like anything other than
Bodies moving, lips, elbows, and knees
And the exchanging of fluids.
But that's what baths are for, I guess.
To get clean.
And her friends keep on dying
So she stays in her bath and weeps as she reads.

miss icarus

Miss icarus
I can't have my love that close to the sun
With all the young dudes that you fuck
When I can't be with you
No
I can't have my love that close to the sun

Miss icarus
Nights out with your girlfriends that you say you don't sleep with
But just that one time
Okay like two times
But like come on
No I can't do that with you
I can't have my love that close to the sun

Miss icarus
Wet wax like cold cum
And the loving of strangers
And all that trust that we never built coming undone
I can't fly that close to your sun
I need my love gentle
I need my love kind
And you say that that's you
And all the rest is just fun
But not for me
The last boring monogamist at the orgy

Miss icarus
Look at what I've become
Be cool
Yeah yeah
Stay cool
I can't imagine you coming for someone
Which is petty and masculine I know
I can't imagine that you would lay that way with them
After all the love we've done

Miss icarus
I can't fly that close to the sun

conversations
with J——(1)

"I feel like a tertiary figure in her life is all."

J—— is sitting across from me, this time we are in Spain.

"What?"

I'm distracted as he speaks. I've been reading about Barbara McClintock's corn study on Wikipedia and haven't been paying attention. No one thought she was smart enough to come up with the concepts she did, so she co-authored the paper with her dog. Sexism is a hell of a drug.

"I don't feel central to her like, fucking life, man."

"Don't be insecure," I tell him sharply, not as softly as I should have. I've been picking at the dirty beach paella between us for 20 mins and it hasn't gotten better.

J—— picks up a fork.

"You're right, being insecure isn't hot."

I gave up on feeling security a long time ago. Maybe I'm defensive of J——'s lover's position because I've made people feel tertiary in my life. Maybe it's the distracted dating of the modern era that's made me tougher. I don't know, I just know I need him to stop being such a little bitch or he isn't going to make it.

"It's not just that being insecure isn't hot, J——, it's that it's sort of like, *abusive*, man."

I don't know what I'm saying.

I am just trying to feel something and at the moment the feeling I'm after is the sacrosanct self-righteousness of a man speaking without actually knowing what the fuck he is talking about. Masculinity is a hell of a drug.

"It's, like, sort of making your shit her problem. It's actually selfish to be insecure; it's sort of like a passive-aggressive violent act, man."

J—— puts down his fork.

I wouldn't say he was stunned but he has gone quiet. This reminds me I'm speaking to someone who takes my opinion very seriously and I should think about what the fuck I'm saying.

"You think?" J's eyes are basically watering. "I'd hate to be bumming her out."

Fuck you, you big softy.

She doesn't deserve you. And I definitely don't deserve you. You are sweet and big-hearted and dumb and beautiful and I want nothing harmful to ever befall you. The little boy inside me wishes I could be this pure. Alas. The rum and the lash. And all the million other things. Like a river ran through. Eroding the rocks into canyons. Leading with your heart is a luxury of the stupid or the brave.

"Sorry. Maybe you aren't like, being *abusive*, man, but you being insecure isn't gonna make her love you more."

Because that is true.

Society says people being vulnerable is revolting. Being open about what makes you feel less-than makes us sick. Insecurity isn't hot. And yet. I don't want him to ever lose that. His insecurity means he is all the way fucking in. And what a rare and lovely thing that is.

"But like, just let her know you don't want to be tertiary, she might have a roster, but you want to be the top of that roster."

J—— pauses again. Deeper and longer than the first time.

"What do you mean by roster?"

Fuck.

bent over, staring at your navel like a narcissist

Slowly sliding in the bath I think about the nature of relaxation,
of "self-care,"
the performance of it.
I can't get comfortable slowly sliding in the bath.
My penis, floating to the surface like a buoy.
I can't relax.
I check my balls to make sure I'm not dying of some cancer
as I stare at the ceiling slowly sliding in the bath,
performing self-care.
I watch myself from above and I laugh.
Staring down from the ceiling,
I watch myself relax.
Only narcissists take baths.
The bent-over posture of the self-obsessed, starring at your navel,
inspecting yourself.
Showers are the way to go.
People usually read poetry for the same reason they take baths.
For self-reflection.
To relax.
I do it for self-inspection.
Dissection.
I look at my skin in disgust,
cutting it open and having a look under the hood
to see if I'm dying.
Same when I'm writing.
Slowly sliding in the bath.

antinatalism

I didn't know there was going to be so much operational upkeep.
if I had known, I'm not sure I would have done it—
being alive, I mean.
Seriously.
You have to water it
sleep it
feed it
piss it
shave it
bathe it

it never ends.
All for what?
So you can swirl around the world "being"?

I feel like someone has given me a dog I don't really want
    to care for.

the insect fatality forensic department

All the bugs keep dying in my apartment.

I even saw a dead lizard once,
its gizzards displayed on cold concrete like some perverse morgue
    for tiny animals.

The spiders are the worst.
Their eight legs, like hairy tentacles, all curled up into a ball,
    I mistake them for little black threads till it's too late and
    I've smashed them to bits with my fingers' tips.

I have to figure out why they keep dying.
It isn't natural.

Sooner or later it will be the cat, or hell, maybe me.

Curled up into a ball, my bones calcified, face frozen in perpetual
    fear, slain by whatever unnatural horror is causing all this
    casual and unfeeling death.

Maybe it's what I am using to clean.

Who knows what kind of military-grade cleaning solvents I've
    been using on the floors,
maybe the whole damn place should be quarantined, maybe they'll
    call the government and the newspeople and they will all
    stand outside my apartment taking notes as they drag out my
    furniture piece by piece to have it incinerated and I have to live
    out the rest of my days in a white room, tied to a chair, while
    men in hazmat suits spray me naked with a fire hose.

I also can't rule out the idea it might be paranormal as well.
The dead bugs.

Yeah, that might be it, maybe that old voodoo doll I brought
back with me from Peru has some sort of demon in it, put
there by some bone-faced shaman in order to curse rich white
voyeuristic tourists who summer there by killing their pets.

That could make sense.

Either way, there are a lot of dead bugs around.

stream of unconsciousness

this is probably how you get yourself hurt.

fucking around in the firmament.

blowing holes in your brain,

snorting shotguns.

I have two beers in my right coat pocket,

a half-smoked pack of Marlboro Smooths in my hand,

ten 200-mg psilocybin pills in my coat's front breast pocket,

and a small bottle of cognac tucked into my jeans

I say small.

It's about 375 ml

and along with the psilocybin pills and the two beers, if ingested
    all at once, is enough to have me screaming and crying down
    the side of the highway I am currently walking.

I don't have bad trips or terrible drunks normally.

But life hasn't been normal.

bingo. My next book title. *sober sex with strangers and other
    awful ideas.*

I need to get back to doing what it is that made you love me
    in the first place.

which is being on fire.

I thought a fireplace would do.

that we could tend to those flames together.

carefully poking it while it roared in the safety of the stone hearth
    of our home

but instead I burnt the fucking house down.

don't make it out of wood if you don't want it to burn.

anyway, I'm painting again.

and dancing.

and fucking around in the firmament.

maybe I'll move to New York and get serious.

maybe I'll move to London and get sad.

do lizards get cancer?

doesn't matter.

I'd only be angry if you dated someone I admired.

which is petty and masculine. Two things I think very little of.

I have 15 mins before I meet my mum and dad for dinner.

I might get a tattoo while I wait

because I hate being bored

and I love chaos

and I can't tell I'm depressed.

how do you measure something like that?

I haven't showered in a while

and I haven't been sleeping

or maybe I've been sleeping too much.

I think I am going to get a dog.

cool numbers

the lady on the L train is a renowned harpist
famous in the circles that avoid fame
and nameless in a world dying from it
I think she has like 14,000 followers
you know
Cool Numbers
anything over 150,000 is too broad
there lies the world of promoted posts
brand endorsements and follower conversion
plus the people who like your posts start to become less nuanced
they don't even really know what you do
they just like that you look good doing it
"daddy"
under a post of a scientist that specializes in gut bacteria
"slay queen"
under a post of an environmental conservationist discussing
    global heat death

the lady on the L train has the cool numbers
but is broke
she follows like 6 people, none of them famous.
In the harpist world
she is a *name* and that kind of value matters when trying
    to get endorsements,
it verifies whether you have value
they use it to measure your worth as a fucking harpist or
    leatherworker or plumber

how do brands know what niche cello player to collaborate
    with next
if they don't have the cool numbers?
Arby's needs that fucking cellist/fast food crossover money
"We Have the Meats" to the tune of Schubert's Sonata in A minor.

acting like a fireman

I am quitting.
I think being a celebrity isn't for me.
It won't save me when the fires start burning
And I don't feel my art is making the world any brighter.

Plus there is more money to be made in destroying the planet
and streaming.

Complete environmental disaster will hit LA first.
Scorched-earth shit.
I am actually a pretty good fireman.
I volunteer in the small town I live in.
You got to move out of the cities, man,
You know,
Before they are all burnt to a crisp.

I live in a town with 1,000 people in it
With one grocery store
And one traffic light
And one fire station.
I haven't exactly "quit" acting.
I act like a fireman now,
Prepping for the whole fucking thing to go up in flames.
I stand beside it with a fire hose,

Not entirely sure what I am saving.

art is a whore's business

We sat around the odd hours of the evening like prostitutes
    drinking champagne,
Francis Bacon made everyone drink champagne.
We drank and drank but in vain.
We always woke up in the morning
to banging hangovers and back to boring.

We sat around the odd hours of the evening like prostitutes
    drinking champagne,
and just like them we got paid for what we were good at.
Art is a whore's business
full of drunks and desperate types.
But if you know how to make your johns happy
you can make the big money
selling your little spark,
monetizing your magic.
Then you, too, can live like prostitutes drinking champagne,
getting paid for what you're good at.

Sex as competition

Sex as a combat sport

Sex as theater

Sex as therapy

Sex as a window into the soul of god

Sex as a dumb biological imperative

Sex as obscurity

Sex as insecurity

Sex as a means of satisfying addiction

Sex as sobriety

Sex as piety

Sex as godlessness

Sex as an act of violence

Sex as an act of love

Sex as a defense mechanism

Sex as freedom

Sex as release

Sex as forbidden thought

Sex as peace

Sex as conveyance of truth

Sex as honesty

Sex as betrayal

Sex as boredom

Sex as an exploration of the soul

Sex as ego

Sex as vulnerability

Sex as stability

Sex as predictability

Sex as a character flaw

Sex as meaningless
Sex as everything
Sex as deception
Sex as manipulation
Sex as manifestation
Sex as a personal belief system
Sex as a personality trait
Sex as death
Sex as a random idle thought
Sex as a prison of your own making
Sex as a dopamine impulse
Sex as validation
Sex as—

raw data

She looked like if PJ Harvey fucked Naomi Campbell.
'90s titty tank top, low-cut jeans, and piercings.
She is the amalgamation of all the raw sexual data I've received
    since birth,
pages and pages of information making up every desire
    I've ever had.
She is Kylie Minogue in that white dress from that one video
and I can't get you out of my head.
She is Jessica Alba on the cover of *GQ*,
water spilling from her open lips,
simulating spit.
She is laying naked on the floor,
looking like Natalie Imbruglia,
who still lays in my childhood bed.
The stirrings of sexual beginnings.
Never really liked the song.
"Torn."
Like Hope Sandoval and Emily Haines and Laura Marling.
Word porn.
And all the sexual information from my childhood swirling
    around in my head
and my groin.

And you have them too.

These people, moments, gestures that you built your
    sexuality on.
The flip of some guy's hair from a show you liked.
Some boy leaning on a locker.
Combat boots.

Odd to be a part of,
to be honest.
Strange to be that for you.

Now I look at all those people that I used when I was younger
to build who I am,
all that raw sexual data I abused,
all the people behind the development of my desire,
all that muse.
And I get confused.

For I know what it feels like to be used.

farm to table pornography

He was disappointed to find out the man who makes the porn
    he likes is a creep.
No one wants to see how the sausage is made.
The fetishes of an angry little sad man.
Like pink slime in a McDonald's hamburger.
"I don't want people to have to do things they don't want to do."
So then don't watch.
Try the vegan option.
Sex workers making content in their bedrooms.
Like farm-to-table pornography.
It's organic.
Free of pesticides, GMOs, and sexual coercion by proxy.
At least it's meant to be.
Everyone pretends to be organic these days
You are what you eat.

no browsing in the sex shop

No browsing in the sex shop.
No wanking at the orgy.
Either you're in or you're out.
That's what I feel about being alive.
No watching from the sidelines.

love fetish

Don't call me "Daddy."
That kink is worn out.
Everybody's somebody's daddy.
The only real kink left is "I love you."
Say, "I'll never leave you."
That's the last taboo
Look me in my eyes and say that you love me
Even though I know it's not true.

manga legs

All manga legs
And Afro
Streetlights and shadows
Sitting in your bed for days like some Caravaggio
Tableau
Moonlight and tacos
The queer dance parties, drunken skate bars,
And jokes
Except you never could stop crying
Your bedsheets always soaked
With sex and with sadness.
All manga legs
And Afro
And all your friends kept on dying
I'm just so sorry that I couldn't be both
Your lover and your friend
From friend into ghost.

build-a-lover

Build-a-lover
With the go-faster stripes
And talk-back box when I pull your strings
Build-a-lover
And remember,
I am hard on my things
I used to sleep with my favorite bunny every night
I'd squeeze her tight until she broke at the seams
I'd wear out her ears and chew on her wet black nose
You're my favorite toy
With go-faster stripes
And talk-back box when I pull your strings
Build-a-lover

send nudes

Looking for love on my phone.
What kind of people send nudes to celebrities?
All kinds of people, it turns out.
I've seen the inside of so many strangers:
Closeted gay retirees,
Divorcees,
Entire college sororities,
And people, speaking plainly, who are just very unwell.
What do they get out of this? I wonder
As I scroll through their offerings.
Why send them to me?
What a strange parasocial construct.
I like to look at their bedrooms.
See what they have hanging on the walls.
PS5s running on the TV in the background,
Hitachi wands,
and bongs.
I don't know what they expect as a response.
So I don't give one.
I feel like this vague sort of ghost,
This voyeuristic specter,
So I stopped opening my messages.

celebrity sex club

It's hard to be a celebrity in a sex club.
This is a hypothetical situation, of course.
I'd *imagine* it would be hard to be a celebrity in a sex club.
Even with your mask on,
I think you'd be worried someone would recognize your tattoos.
There is no true anonymity anymore.
Which I think is a good thing.
Helps you live honestly.
Hard to lie.
When the whole room is staring at your naked body.

(3)

"It's my grandfather's hat."

This is a lie.

I say it because _____ has stolen my hat and barricaded herself in her room.

It is 5 a.m. and the party is over. To be honest, it has been over for hours, but curious nature, remember? And so I stayed to see what might happen.

What happened is _____ decided she is going to fuck me.

I am 18 and she is much older than me.

_____ used to be famous.

Like really famous.

Before the drinking and the drugs.

Before she stole jewelry from the Dorchester Hotel in London.

Before basically all the adults in her life failed her.

I was a magnet for women like that back then, I think they saw me as someone they would have liked to have dated when they were young. I exemplified the type of boy they were meant to have a crush on, if they had been raised normal. Of course, when they were young, they were with much older men. They all grew up too young, those kids on TV, and I guess I did too, now that I look back at the places I went and the things that I knew.

I was a little different, I think. I was always on the outside. Always watching from just far enough away to not get lost in it. I think that's why I'm okay. My hero at the time was Hunter S. Thompson. I got *buy the ticket, take the ride* tattooed on my ribs when I was seventeen. I got it for The Show. I got it to remind myself that this is the life I chose. Got to ride it out. I admired

Hunter. Make yourself a part of the story. So my job was to just float and feed my curiosity, and I would find myself all types of places. Like tonight, where I found myself knocking on _____'s door at 5 a.m. trying to get my hat back.

"Give me the hat back."

She opens the door slowly.

The little adult girl all grown up into the child-woman.

She just wants to be a teenager again.

She smiles at me, the bright dangerous flicker of white fuck in her eyes.

"Come inside."

And I do.

I get my hat back and immediately leave.

I had a curious nature, not a stupid one.

the boy prostitute to the stars

American teen gigolo.

Boy prostitute to the stars!

We fuck in her offices normally. Because it's away from her kids and because she is the boss, so we can meet there after hours. Also, it is obviously very hot to have sex in that environment. Her offices are in the big white building on La Cienega or maybe Sepulveda, I have decided to forget the exact location to protect her identity.

To be clear, she isn't *my* boss. So there are no abuses of power here except for maybe she likes me to take control, even though I am 19 and she is "older." It's indiscreet to mention a woman's age. Mostly because society devalues woman over a certain number. 37. If you are wondering.

is this how a heartthrob is meant to act?

Is this how a heartthrob is meant to act?
Out every night,
Drunk,
Single and fuckable,
Unapproachable and unattainable.
Why aren't you like that?
What's wrong with you?
"If I was you, I'd fuck everything that moved."
Men have told me this in so many different ways
And women too.
You are meant to act like a heartthrob, Avan.
So why don't you?
I think I got trapped
Acting like a heartthrob.
Not to say I haven't done a good job of it.
I am, after all, an actor.
But it has always felt cumbersome and odd.
The sweater is itchy and hot.
I'd rather be alone.
I think I give the game away as soon as I open my mouth.
'Cause the heartthrob is not meant to speak.
When I talk and laugh and am silly and then very sad
It gives too much life away.
You can't project your own personal version of a heartthrob
    onto me.
Stand there, look pretty, and smile.
So they can fantasize about who they've decided you are
    for a while.

standing at the mirror, running my lines

I find it hard to not view myself without intense vanity
And therefore, with intense dissatisfaction.
I am standing staring in a mirror running lines.
I observe the slope of my eyes
And the strong heavy arch of my nose.
I look like an actor stuck in a pose.
I've been in so long my bones and joints have all closed.
Stiff with uncertainty.
I don't like this show,
The one I'm auditioning for.
I can't remember the lines.
Some fucking thing about a lawyer or a doctor.
Some fuckable brown side character to a bland, unremarkable lead.
I can't remember the words 'cause I don't know what they mean.
None of the words have any fucking meaning.
I wish for a war worthy of my life.
That's all the actor wants,
To be a well-used tool.
I stare at my eyes,
Bloodshot and yellowing.
I can't tell if it's the light in here but my skin looks all gray.
I can feel the skin sliding down my face as I age.
When I was younger I couldn't wait
To be weathered and old,
So that maybe I could be a real actor,
You know,
In films that were worthy of sacrificing my soul.
This is its own kind of vanity.
Not concerned with grace or looking a certain way
But concerned with being a bright talented thing.

This poem itself
Is an act of vanity.
Look at the actor,
All sad and morose.
Such a dramatic and self-involved species.
My life is great.
I'm a ghost.
My life is great.
I'm a ghost.
Staring into the bathroom mirror,
Haunting my host.

fan mail

She actually answers fan mail
She spent 6 hours doing it.
I think she is meant to do this.
Have fans, I mean,
I might answer a message you send me online,
Some weird thing I thought was funny,
Or show up unannounced to your local basement party,
Or sit and talk with you on the side of the road.
I am meant to roam,
To be caught in the wild.
Keanu Reeves.
I am meant to have admirers that want to share in the secret,
Create strange moments together.
Plus my handwriting is garbage and slow.
She has that lovely swoopy writing of a teacher's pet.
She will answer you if you write to her,
She will ask you about your college plans
And if you are still dating that hot guy in your dorm.
Personal.
She remembers and is interested in you.
I am not that kind of celebrity.
I am impressed every day by her.
The care and tender heart that when she isn't writing you letters
Puts her tiny little hand in mine.
She loves you all.
Truly.
I am a cynic.
Grumpy mostly.
She is too good for this world
And for me.
And most probably for you.

like rats on a sinking ship

Who cares what a celebrity has to say.
I'm tired of being asked my fucking opinion on everything.
Who cares what I think.
"You have a voice."
Maybe I don't like what I have to say.
Maybe I just take up space.
Ask an activist
or a scientist.
Maybe Jason Derulo doesn't have the hard-hitting, evidence-based
    information I need on global conflict.
When did we care so much what entertainers think?
Sure, I can get online and echo-chamber out some expert's
    opinion on climate change, but for what?
To have people comment "slay bestie" under it?
Or fucking hate me?
What have I changed?
This is a legitimate question I'm asking.
I am not trying to be vague or coy.
I want to know what an actor can do about our global spiritual
    impoverishment
and humanity's moral decay.
"Make art,"
is what you're supposed to say,
but it just sounds so fake.

The *Titanic* is sinking and we are asking the fucking violinists
    to help plug the holes.

While the captain and crew of the ship are already in the lifeboats,
pushing out the women and children.

I'm just a violinist, I don't steer the boat.

scroll

Middle Eastern refugees, faceless effigies
nailed to our feed.
Scroll

An ad for a new eyewear brand.
Scroll

The dismembered body of a child.
Scroll

You won't believe what Britney did this time.
Scroll

cat video.
Scroll

2 hours have gone by
and now I'm watching Pandora do an unboxing video on
    YouTube.
I realize I haven't posted anything about all the conflict.
    I should, right?
Some . . . endorsement of some kind? Or condemnation?
And even as I'm typing this I think,
"What the fuck am I doing?!
"I should be out there helping! Throwing bags of rice off
    a fucking helicopter or something!"
Scroll

The theme for the Met Gala this year is a blinding lack
    of perspective.
Scroll

Your post doesn't help, you say. People are still dying.
There is a global death cult
and its members are the leadership of every government on earth.
The shifting of the tectonic plates of industry and conquest
     way beyond your control,
us, the people, helplessly falling into the cracks.
"This is the way of things," you tell yourself.

You are a shit shoveler, from generations of shit shovelers.
Know your place.
You are a spineless, feckless little coward
and you won't do a fucking thing till they come knocking on
     your door.
Then, of course,
it will be too late, You are no Sophie Scholl.
Scroll

it's important to die in a cool way

They say fame is immortality
But it's not really.
Sure, you are remembered after you are dead and gone
But it's not really you.
Some fucking cardboard cutout,
Some dollar-store James Dean,
Marilyn Monroe gift shop knockoff.
And that's only if you matter enough for them to sell your useless
    junk after you kick the bucket.
In order to matter after your death,
Firstly, your death must be untimely.
Old people dying isn't interesting.
Any age over 37, who cares?
Second, you also have to die in a really fun and engaging way,
Like an airplane crash
Or an overdose.
Cancer isn't gonna cut it.
It's gotta be evocative and unique.
Everyone dies of cancer.
Boring.
Gotta die doing something that normal people don't do.
Wrapping a silver Porsche around a tree at 140 miles an hour.
Deciding you don't need the parachute when you go skydiving.
Having a heart attack at a cocaine-fueled orgy.
Something cool.
And the third thing you have to do to be remembered, and this
    is less important than the dying young or cool,
Is you have to have made something that moves people.

Some piece of art that resonates with the collective soul
     of humanity,
Some garden of work left on earth that nurtures the generations
     to come.
But again,
Not as important as dying young and in a cool way.

born again

I am smoking outside a club that hasn't opened yet. I am in
　　Peckham or Clapham or Shoreditch or Dalston. It is 7 p.m.
　　and the first act goes on at 9. I am smoking in a lavender coat,
　　mehndi covering my hands, staring at my fingernails.

"Hello?"
I turn to see a 20-something Nigerian girl with vibrant, searching
　　eyes, looking at me.
"Oh, hi," I reply.
"What's your name?" she asks.
"A-Avan."

I hesitate when I say this, because sometimes I lie. I wince and
　　prepare myself for what I assume is the inevitable "I grew up
　　watching you on TV."

She smiles. "Are you born again? Do you know god? Do you
　　believe?"
Not everyone wants a fucking photo, Avan.
Some people just want to corner you outside nightclubs and talk
　　about their lord and savior.

I find myself thankful she only wants to peddle her religion and
　　that she doesn't, in fact, want a photo to show her friends. "Oh,
　　I feel I know god," I say. "Really!" She beams at me. Her bright
　　eyes wet and shining with the glory of revelation, I assume,
　　that or a chemical imbalance.

"Or like *gods*. I am a Hindu." And I show her my hands, covered in
　　mehndi. Sometimes I lie.

I'm about as Hindu as the killing floor of a cattle ranch. Although I've been more religious recently. But I felt silly trying to defend against the might of her religious fervor with my petty little "spiritual beliefs." My pathetic little "intuitions." What good are those in the face of 2,000 years of organized horror, death, ecstasy, and wonder?

"Oh," she responds. The light in her eyes doesn't fade but changes: she knows now what she must do. She has her orders, by god, her lord, to deliver to heaven the sinners and heathens and smokers outside nightclubs, who wear lavender coats and believe in false idols.

Tonight, I am the unwashed and godless.
And she is Joan of fucking Arc.

my mother on a bobsled

It is winter and a little girl pulls her bobsled up the biggest hill
    in Jenner, Alberta,
which isn't saying much, as Alberta is quite flat.

This is no normal girl.
This girl thinks big thoughts.
She worries about earthquakes underwater and if dogs think
    our clothes look silly.
She worries about if there is enough salt or if at some point
    we will run out.
She worries about her parents and wonders what they will do
    without her.

But as she lines up her sled and pushes herself off down the hill,
all her big thoughts leave her.
Blind in the bliss of a white blizzard.
She is free. She is just feeling without awareness.
That perfect moment of nothingness, brain and body simply
    being, without consciousness,
as her face is beaten red by the whipping wind.

This moment doesn't last, it is small and beautiful as moments
    of truth always are.
As she picks up speed, all her big thoughts come rushing back
    to her.
Although she has one thought that she hasn't had before.
"What if I am the second coming of Christ?"

The feeling that comes to her after that thought
isn't the joyous religious euphoria of being filled with the lord.
But rather this little girl, clutching desperately to her red bobsled,
feels she is now responsible for the whole human race.

All of the gas prices,
the wars she doesn't understand,
the evil, hateful, awful things that humans do to each other
    and themselves.
The parking situation.
Inflation, which again she doesn't understand.
All of it was now her problem.

And in that very instant she felt a wave of fear,
having felt the weight of all things, made and unmade,
upon her little shoulders.
Like boulders, like boulders, like boulders.
Then she stopped,
for a second thought had entered her mind.
Doubt.
So human, it cast her first thought out.
She wasn't, in fact, the second coming of Christ.
'Cause if she was, she imagined, she would never have any doubt.
And she would know what to do about the parking situation.
She is just a human girl, born with a big brain, in the age of doubt.
Who doesn't know.
"what if I am not good enough?"
"what if I am not good enough?"
"what if I am not good enough?"
and then she was buried in snow.

little bird

Forget what you're told.
Remember, little bird,
love is just time
that's grown old.
So hold your head on my chest
and please do your best
to let me hold you.

See, because time's getting on,
and you know how I feel about time
and the things that it's done.
The things that we do
end up what we become,
so let me become you.

Forget what you're told.
Remember, little bird,
love is just time
that's grown old.
So hold my hand as we walk
and maybe we will talk
and I'll pass the time
with you.

sweating in your sleep

Little hard breaths on my shoulder
Roll over
Let me hold you
All small and limp
Sweat on your forehead
Sleeping hard and pretty
On top of my body
So dense
My hand pats the back of your head
Kissing the sweat off your brow
All salty and flowery
A short little sigh
To show me you're no longer tense
Good night, little bird,
Relax and just rest.

your face unrevealing.

You're lying in your childhood room
on the bed next to me, gazing up at the ceiling.
From my angle, your eyes look like starlight
as you watch your wallpaper peeling.

And I infer feeling.

The humid, sweaty, white paint window
is stuck open from the salt water and the heat.
And the breeze coming in from the ocean
smells like juniper leaves and clean sheets.

And it implies meaning.

I go to touch you but my fingertips are cold
and my breath is hot and you push me away.
And the smell of juniper leaves is gone
and so is your starlight
and the clouds have gone gray.

Your face unrevealing,
so I infer feeling.

golden leaf

I had a dream that you were lying on the sofa by the bed,
shoulders heavy,
fingers grasping for what was inside my head,
for words I was not saying,
words that would not ever let you rest.
Your weary eyes are fading.
Falling fast is probably for the best.

Golden leaf,
I see you shining in the grass on the lawn,
outside the love
that I tried.

The soil is wet in your garden.
Please do pardon my regret.
Our flowers wilt,
for they are built on paper napkins of my pretend.
Your pretty breeze
will bring the petals to their knees.
In the end,
we will be what we will be.

Golden leaf,
I see you shining in the grass on the lawn,
outside the love
that I tried.

sugar packet

I only use half the sugar packet.
I don't know when I started doing that.
Some silly performance of restraint.
I wonder what other ways I wait,
what other things I go half in on,
how much I've done at pace
rather than running fast and straight.
Using half the sugar packet.
It's not even about my weight.
It's about not taking up too much space.
Half measures.
As if you'd ever succeed in life
practicing restraint.

ezra

I almost drown in the ocean with a boy named Ezra one summer,
I was 19.
We wouldn't die that day.
I remember tossing in the waves on the coast of the world,
thrown adrift by the drag and the sway of the sea of infinity.
And I thought I could die.
Not that I didn't believe I could.
We can, all of us, always die
but I felt I could want to die
as the shore drifted farther away
and Ezra even farther out than me.

But a foot from the brink
of the waterfall into nothing,
the waves broke and brought us both back to shore.

Me first,
Ezra second.

I remember grabbing him and asking if he was okay.
He said he was.
And he was.

He would die two years later.
Brain aneurysm.
Unknowable and unpredictable.
And I would remember the time we both almost drowned
      in the ocean one summer.

And I would wonder why it wasn't me.

the responsibility of consciousness

I go to my dog as the lightning flashes through our living room
    window.
Knowing the thunder that comes after will frighten him.
I kiss his head and stroke just under his neck.
So that when the thunder comes, he may have comfort.

This is the responsibility of consciousness.
To comfort those who don't know what the lightning brings.

well worn

He was the kind of man who was hard on his things.
He was hard on his cars.
The brakes would blow after a year.
Or he'd change gears too rough
and drop the clutch out of it.
His boots always get worn out at the heel earlier than they should.
He'd stomp around so much the whole sole would come out.
He was also hard on his women.
Not saying he'd smack 'em around or anything horrible like that.
He was just hard on them.
It was hard to be his woman.
He'd wear you out
like the heel of his boot.
Or be too rough on you
like when he changes gears.
It was hard to be his woman.
But he used his things well.
And it's nice to be used well.
Maybe not with care.
But used fully
and loved.
'Cause he loves that broken, used-up car
and his well-worn boots
and his woman.

sonnet to my woman's lover

Heard you treated my woman like a stranger.
Heard you loved her
and you laid her.
Heard you sent some red roses
up to her new apartment.
Heard you called her
and you wrote her.
Heard about the gifts that you gave her.
Heard that you,
my only brother,
asked if you could come and claim her.

And what's worst is
I heard you treated her right.

Heard you bathed her
and you made her
into a baby in a manger.
Gave her the sharp prick of new love
that my loving had forbade her.
Heard you loved her,
really loved her,
my cold and ruined lover.
You renewed her
and you pulled her
from the rubble she was under.

So I thank you.
Yes, I thank you.
My brother, now I task you
with loving her in all the ways
that she's going to ask you.

the saddest girl at the party, standing by the punch bowl

Selfishly "protecting my peace"
Love for lease
Your heart on a leash
Protection at the cost of being lonely
The saddest girl at the party,
standing by the punch bowl
Yeesh
The trade-off for never hurting
Radical individualism
No one can get in the way of your good time.
"Remove toxic people from your life."
Instagram therapists trying to free you of your guilt
and by virtue of that
free you from your humanity
The saddest girl at the party,
standing by the punch bowl
by herself,
alone and free

cheering for the bad guys

I'm at the bar and the patrons are watching a high-speed car chase
    on the TV
and they're cheering for the bad guys,

And someone is singing "Copacabana" on a karaoke machine.
But no one is listening.
And then my beautiful friend with rainbow hair starts singing
"Nothing Compares 2 You."
And then people listen.
And I am wearing your mother's Hawaiian-print shirt.
And I am drinking mai tais
And I am drunk
And I've been drunk for days.

And you are gone.
Not because you left,
Or I did,
But because we hadn't time left.

And a voice sings Kenny Rogers
And I dance a samba
And the people watch the car chase and cheer for the bad guys,
I guess 'cause the bad guys don't always start out that way
And they can see themselves behind the wheel.

"It's all fun and games till someone gets shot in the head,"
Is what I say about love.

"It's all fun and games till you're behind bars,"
Is what I say about marriage.

And I am not singing karaoke tonight.
I've lost my voice.

conversations with J——(2)

"It hurt a lot,"

J—— says, as I sit across from him at coffee. He stares at me. Maybe not at *me* but at some faraway thing, beyond me. I just happen to be in his eyeline.

"What was it like?" I ask, rather stupidly.

"Unpleasant." he replies obviously, and yet pauses for a moment, as if to say more.

But doesn't.

If I was to hazard a guess at what the pause was for, I'd say it was because as unpleasant as it was, as challenging to his peace as it was, it felt good, really good, to be back with her again.

"It was the laughing that got to me." He has finally turned his gaze away from me to watch a kid walk by with an ice cream.

It's sunny, but it's always sunny. We are sat outside a coffee shop on Franklin Blvd in LA. I used to live right by here. This used to be my coffee shop, actually. I used to love their lattes, but it's a different coffee shop now.

A lot has changed, some things not for the better.

Maybe it's not fair to judge change as it's happening. Maybe it's only hindsight that offers the proper context. Even then, memory warps things, distends and distorts, blurring joy and pain. Now that I think about it, I'm not sure their lattes were anything special.

"I guess I just didn't expect to hear us laughing. I always felt there was so much conflict all the time, you know?" He continues on. "And like, I am used to the aching pain that has become sort of like a stone in my shoe that I've grown to walk with. . . .

"But when I heard the laughing . . . it was sharp, man, the pain, it wasn't a dull ache. It was a gut punch. I lost my breath for a second."

He goes quiet. I know that kind of quiet, it's a kind a quiet that comes from guilt and loss. The kind of quiet that worms its way into the back of your mind, and no matter how much noise you make to drown it out, it whispers, tongue wet with poison.

"What if?"

It's weird when you are the author of your own loss. Where nothing has been taken from you so much as you have given it away. It's weird when you put the stone in your own shoe willingly.

"Anyway," he says, "if your iCloud is full, just pay the $3.99 for more storage . . . don't go back and delete your old videos and shit."

ode to sylvia plath

Sylvia Plath doesn't get enough play
or whatever.
Maybe she gets *too much* play
but she was great.
"The brute brute heart of a brute like you."
God, I love you,
you brilliant dead old young lady.
I want to live in your mind like a parasite.
You eat men like air,
you brilliant dead old young lady,
you hare.
Words jumping up and down on the page.
"Head in the freakish Atlantic where it pours bean green over blue."
Fuck you.
That line so slick like an oil spill on my tongue.
I want to fuck you,
to be some lover you hated,
to be some line.
What a selfish and small little desire.
"Every woman adores a Fascist."
To be that for you.
Bless you,
you brilliant dead old young lady.
I listen to you read your poems on YouTube.
Your long upper-crust drawl
and the crackle of consonants.
You are god's forgotten woman.
I pin your poems up on my wall the way people pin the posters
    of pop stars.
You brilliant dead old young lady,
I love you.

if you aren't cool, I can't come

Up late at night at the Met,
masturbating to Alfred Stieglitz's nude photographs of
   Georgia O'Keeffe,
she listens to "Ballade de Melody Nelson" till climax.
Obscure references as foreplay.
Art fucking.
I'm cooler than you 'cause I know all the names of the things
   that are cool.
"If you aren't cool, I can't come,"
she whispers at the Musée de l'Orangerie in Paris
as she wets the sex towel in her Marcel Duchamp *Fountain* replica.
Art fucking.

alabaster

I see her in the bathroom alabaster.
as she slides her panties to the floor.
I remember how I felt the moment after,
knowing I've never felt that way before.

How did I think that I could ever be her master,
when she comes to me in such a perfect form?
How could any man demand the moments after,
when she comes to me, in this, her purest form?

I see her in the bathroom alabaster
as she picks her panties off the floor.
Now I know no man could ever be her master
and I'm no different than the ones that came before.
I am no different than all the others who've come before.

hidden ace

I know this type of game,
the kind that's ruled by sin and stains.
She plays it well
but she is playing with a master.

I know the cards she plays,
the hidden ace.
I've played so much it seems
with every card
I know just what she's after.

How can she be so pretty as a lover
and yet be so ugly as a master?

maybe I'm not what you're looking for

She sat there watching *Belle de Jour*
and asked me to call her a whore
and I can, if you really want me to.
But I won't mean it.
Not in the way you want.
I can fake it pretty good
but what you're looking for can't be fucked into you.

bald spot

I have a bald spot under my chin where you used to pet me.
Oh, how you have kept me
Under lock and key
For you.
I love my golden cage, baby.
I love my ruby collar too.
Keep me in my gilded prison
Where all I can do
Is be in love with you.
Use me for sex and validation.
Keep me kept
And true.

you never seem to get sore

His love struck you dumb
"Baby come hit me"
You never seem to get sore
His love knocked you backwards
Off of your feet
Clean off the sheets
To the floor
His love took the wind right out of your lungs
Wheezing and coughing
And brainless and dumb
Until love struck you numb
Till you couldn't feel it anymore
Till the punches felt blank
Strong jaw
You never seem to get sore

the fascist dictator

The fascist dictator
The lover
With his black boot on your neck
And you
In your beautiful crown
And gilded chains
It is the job of the woman to suffer
That's how your lover feels
He wants you to know pain and obedience
He wants to own your freedom
He buys it with kind words
and the lies of an angel
He buys it for cheap
and sells it for fortunes
Solomon blushes at the purse made from your prison
For your belief in him is more precious than gold
formed from fickle metals
The fascist dictator prides himself on his power over you
Because with you he has won a most valuable prize
The trust of a woman.

. . .

can you do me no harm?
or at least known harm
hurt me like I am used to, baby,
break my body with your charm
hit me with your instability
carve your initials in my arm
I'll bear you children if you'd like, baby,
god I love it when you're calm
god I love it when you don't respond
. . .
in your reply
god I love it when you're gone
god I love all of your red flags, babe,
I'm in love with your alarms

hunchbacks of the hollywood hills

I am that haunted hunchback
I am the fiendish horde
I roam the hills and valleys
searching only for the lord

instead I find Him in the gutter
and I find Him in the bars

I find Her in my bedroom chamber
And I find Her in the stars

I swing from candelabras in the halls
of Californian castles

I've been nailed to effigies of actresses
I've drank flames and snorted ashes

I am that hateful wasteful hunchback
Chewing charcoal and drinking acid

I am your erected dirty desire, babe,
I am your moral compass, flaccid

idle worship

The idle worship of the faithless.
The herd of lazy sheep.
Disciples don't believe in you as much as they used to.
Sort of takes the fun out of being the messiah.
Preachers preach
to a room full of gods.
Makes a priest want to give up the ghost.
Jesus was the original heartthrob.
Whenever I see him on the cross I think,
"I wonder what his ab workout was?"
Who'd want to be a fan when everyone's a star?
Slaughtered sheep.
Hard to gather devout apostles for the feast
when everyone's dad is god.
Look at all of us.
So many tiny upstart religions.
All these heathens
golden fleeced.
A new belief system.
Idle worship.
The only god left is you and me.

wikipedia funeral

A famous actress died 11 minutes ago and the internet wept
    and wept.
I got to her Wikipedia page before it had been updated with news
    of her death.
Felt like I was watching a funeral of sorts.
Refresh refresh.
I took a screen grab so I had the evidence that she had once lived
before her page referred to her in the past tense.
Bye-bye, famous actress.
Never saw a film you acted in.
Bye-bye, beloved actor.
You died in your house, fridge open.
You had a heart attack.
What a way to die.
What a way to live.
Get sober and blow away
cocaine for a decade.
Human decay.
So silly.
I just refreshed her Wiki page.
She is dead now.
Officially.

storage facility poem (1)

This storage facility that I am at in the valley is busy,
Very fucking busy.
"Damn, is it like National Storage Day?"
Ron, the man who works the counter, whispers to himself.
Everyone has lost their ID and everyone is angry.
There is a white millennial man,
red-faced, spittle cascading from his mouth,
yelling into his phone as he leaves,
"Just listen to me, shut up, do exactly as I say, you need to get here
    because I don't have my ID and you need ID to rent the space."
And everyone is dumping their dreams here.
There is an old Hispanic couple storing cheap plywood furniture
    from IKEA
and a young black guy is moving in with his girlfriend,
so he needs to leave some stuff here.
He seems hopeful at least.
And it reeks of the chaos of new beginnings.
And someone wheels in a 7-foot wooden horse
and Ron says,
"Yo man, I told you, you need to get that thing out of here."
And the man with the wooden horse turns it around,
and the millennial comes back in.
And he has calmed down
and he apologizes to the room for losing his cool
and we all nod and forgive him.

storage facility poem (2)

Everything I've ever owned is buried in a storage facility
under the 101 freeway in Hollywood.
All my thoughts and feelings and beliefs.
All my grief.
I am keeping it in case of need of use.
In case I get too comfortable and have nothing to write about.
What an awful day.
I feel like we relish in pain,
use it as fuel,
use it for gain,
but I have stored all my pain away,
buried in a storage facility under the 101 freeway in Hollywood
in case I get too comfortable.
What a strange and awful day.
But like most things in storage,
I could probably just throw it away
and be okay.

the billionaires are going to burn the celebrities

The billionaires are going to burn the celebrities
Like sacrificial lambs.
They know you're upset.
The billionaires.
They can see you getting angrier every day.
With the marching and the boycotting and the carrying on.
And they don't want you blaming *them*, for god's sake.
That'd be terrible.

So they are going to burn the celebrities.

"Look at them!"
"They are rich and excessive!"
And that *is* true.
Celebrities, with our exhausting self-involvement.
Our holier-than-thou opinions and endorsement deals.
We are just *so* fucking annoying.

But celebrities aren't the reason you can't pay your rent.
Or that you don't have health care
Or that you're in student loan debt
Or that you will never be able to buy a house.

To the billionaire, celebrities are just jesters.
Simply there for entertainment.
Easy to buy.
Easy to burn.
Some of us, although not many, even come from the lower classes.
So like two birds, one stone.

They will burn us first and hope you are satisfied.
And if you aren't,
they'll burn the whole world
rather than fucking treat you as human.

adaptive evolution

Did you know that earwigs have evolved to look like AirPods
    in order to more easily burrow into your ears?*
Look it up.
It's called adaptive evolution.
When a creature develops a new evolutionary trait to respond
    to changes in its environment.
Got to move with the times.
Like microbacteria learning to eat plastic in the ocean
Or in your gut.
Got to keep up with a changing world.
Adapt.
That is the great measure of success in a species.
At least as it pertains to survival.
I know of no known metric by which to measure the kind
    of success
That concerns itself with beauty, love, or things or worth.
But to be successful in survival you have to adapt.

Like the earwig
Or the microbacteria.
I've tried to adapt
To this ever-changing environment.
But I've found I lack the survival instinct.
Things are different and worse.
I feel old and off track.
I don't concern myself with even trying to adapt,
The first sign of a dying species.
What good, I think, is survival.
Especially having seen what new limbs I'd have to grow
To make it in this new world.

A soft and malleable mandible
So I can unhinge my jaw and swallow the earth.
What is the point of adapting to survival
If it evolves you away from things of worth?

*This is a lie, don't worry.

i am on set getting yelled at

I am on set getting yelled at. I am still a teenager, and I am shaking with rage. The kind of quiet anger that makes you change. I should thank him, probably. But right now, he is embarrassing me, and I am fucking up my lines.

Never give someone who was bullied in high school power.

The year is firmly 2010. As proof of this, Ke$ha is on set today. TikTok hadn't been invented, yet I think this is her big song at the moment. Why she is singing about "brushing her teeth with a bottle of Jack" on a kids' show is unknown to me. Besides, I am having my own problems today. I can't say Ke$ha's fucking name. I keep on fucking up my line. "No, check out Kee$ha's last update!" I am tired, I am hungover, and I am bored. I am always far too easily bored.

I have never been able to do things I'm not passionate about. I can fake it for a time, but then people start to notice, or I just give up entirely. Not a great trait in an actor, really. Being an actor is about getting smacked in the face and happily turning your cheek asking for more. Not for me. Acting is a submissive enterprise, and although I have a big ol' hole in my heart, I don't need to fill it with the kind of validation one gets from the adoration of strangers. That doesn't fill my cup. I need the adoration of my peers and people I respect, that golden ambrosia of feeling included among people I consider truly brilliant. I don't want to seem as if I am positioning that as a nobler cause, it is still pretty pathetic, but I bring it up to say that the opinion of people I don't respect means very little to me.

Which means I must have respected him. In a way. For him to
make me so angry that I could cry. To let him embarrass me like
that. I was young enough that my anger was bright and panicked.
Your anger becomes steady the older you get, but back then it
was urgent. And I can't get my fucking line right. "No, check out
Kee$ha's last update!"

He has gotten up. He never gets up from his chair. Mostly he
calls out from the inky darkness of the soundstage. Shows like
this usually shoot with a studio audience; ours didn't probably on
account of how much he liked to control his little kingdom. Also,
you can't yell at people with a studio audience watching. He walks
over to me in front of everyone and says,

"Hey, Avan, do my checks clear?"

"Huh?"

"The checks I send you every week, do they clear?"

"Yeah . . ."

"Then say the line right."

the first poem I ever wrote

I am just a teenager.
I am compelled to raise hell.
It lives in my veins like a burning thing I can't fit straight.
Young, dumb, and full of come, I find homes inside others.
Not people, but things.

The mindlessly fuck-able and easily chuck-able.
Living organisms share orgasms as their organs meet.
Beat down by high school, a pool of fools.
Who answer to lawmakers and life takers.

but I am just a teenager.

I find solace in mushrooms and vacant rooms
full of furniture no one can see but me,
and in the moment
I pretend to be
a child again.
But I can't go back,
innocence lost, the cost, is higher than payout,
a dreary layout,
a future full of minimum wage and takeout.

but I am just a teenager.

A comatose state,
late for science class, out by the dumpster for a smoke break,
it fills my lungs like some kind of biological warfare,
but I don't care,
I won't dare,
for the fear of being "uncool."

I am a teenager.

Apathy rules the world I see,
and as we cut our wrists for attention
we make mention
to some band whose lyrics speak to our souls.

I am teenager.

I laugh at violence on television,
numb to the struggles of the world,
too concerned with fucking girls,
hurling as the world curls, and life unfurls,

Towers burn and the economy falls,
but I'm busy, standing tall, thinking with my balls,
and answering telephone calls,
on my cellular mobile phone,
while people struggle for food in mobile homes.

I am just a teenager.

Self-centered and self-righteous,
feeling like I might just
start a revolution from this computer screen,
a gutter dream,
like some scene from a movie that you've never seen.
Or place you've never been.

I am a teenager.

I worship dead rock icons as gods
and choose a life of drugs and destruction
rather than a safe bachelor's degree in construction,
and yes I will take that tax reduction,
and yes I will take those drugs to function,
and yes I will take a left at the next junction
just because the navigation told me to,

but what can I do?

I am just a teenager.